22 And the Mother of 11

An Alaska Frontier Instant Mother's Story

by

Betty Epps Arnett

For Jim —
KHS classmate! —
Enjoy — Betty Epps
Arnett
my

 PUBLICATION
CONSULTANTS
We Believe In The Power Of Authors

PO Box 221974 Anchorage, Alaska 99522-1974
books@publicationconsultants.com—www.publicationconsultants.com

ISBN 978-1-59433-695-9
eBook ISBN Number: 978-1-59433-696-6

Library of Congress Catalog Card Number: 2017937562

Copyright 2017 Betty Epps Arnett
-First Edition-

Manufactured in the United States of America.

To my C Boys from 1952-54.

ACKNOWLEDGEMENTS

Much of this book is based on information given to me by DOLORES MOREY STEAD of her life at Jesse Lee Home, as a former housemother for the C Girls and later the B Boys in Seward, Alaska from 1952-1954. Her generosity in sharing that material has allowed me to weave both of our experiences to create *22 and the Mother of 11*. I hope I have displayed her wonderful sense of humor that kept us all going.

As a young, single woman new to Alaska and new to parenting, VIRGINIA SEARCH KIRK became a housemother for the B Girls at the Jesse Lee Home in Seward from 1953-55. Jenny gave me much encouragement and material from her own experience, which helped in creating this book.

STEVE BROOKS and I were members of the Storytelling Delegation to South Africa in the People to People Ambassador Program in 2004. To my luck, Steve just happened to be an adjunct professor of creative writing at the University of Central Florida, and graciously consented to read my manuscript in its early beginnings. With his guidance, the content took a different path and became less a report and more of a memoir. He gave me much encouragement and convinced me I could write.

JUDITH CONTE was an instructor in a Memoir Writing Class provided by the "49 Writers," an organization in Alaska that promotes creative writing. She is an excellent teacher and offered to read my entire manuscript. Afterwards, she insisted it was ready and that I should find a publisher.

At the end of JUDITH CONTE'S Memoir Writing class, a few of us began to meet on Saturdays for a short while to continue critiques on our writing. The following people gave me much support and good direction in completing my manuscript: ANNETTE ALLEVA, JEANNE ASHCRAFT, GARY ROGERS, SUSAN ROGERS, AND SHIRLEY SCHNEIDER.

"Chapter Parties" were held in my home, as I would feel a chapter had been brought to completion. I would send chapters to people in the community, whose opinions I respected and knew they would give me constructive feedback. Some had been high school English teachers, and some were writers themselves. From their critiques, my chapters were greatly improved. Thanks to LORETTA CURGUS, RENEE DOWNS, HANNAH FRENIER, MARGARET GINGERICH, KAREN INGRAHAM, MAXINE RADER, and MILLIE SPEZIALY.

Thanks to my two brilliant daughters, APRIL ARNETT and HEATHER ARNETT, who read parts of the manuscript and gave me excellent advice in composition, punctuation, and grammar. Thanks also to my son, HANS ARNETT, for all of his interest and support.

PREFACE

Jesse Lee Home has been taking care of children in Alaska for over one hundred years and has existed in three different locations:
Unalaska in the Aleutian Islands, 1890-1925,
Seward on the Kenai Peninsula, 1925-1966, and
Anchorage in South Central Alaska 1966 - ?

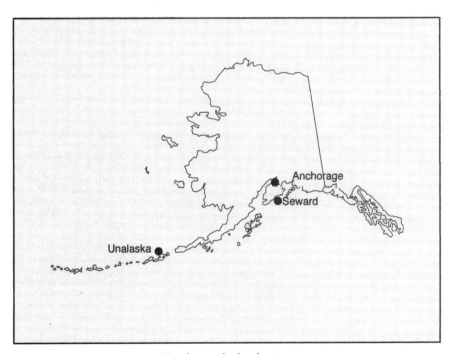

Map showing the three locations.

JESSE LEE HOME IN UNALASKA

Twenty years after the purchase of Alaska from Russia, the Agent for Education, Dr. Sheldon Jackson, saw the need for an industrial school in western Alaska. Knowing it would take a missionary zeal to persevere in this new territory, he sought the Methodists to construct the institution and to send an educational missionary. The government would offer housing and salary.

Orphaned girls arrived in Unalaska without a place to stay and John Tuck, a missionary from Connecticut, and his wife, had to take them into their small house, while waiting for construction to begin. Numbers grew. Out of desperation, Tuck pleaded for another missionary. Agnes Sowle arrived. By 1900 the first building was completed; the Tucks had left; and Agnes successfully offered to split her salary of $30.00 a month with Miss M.E. Mellor, if she would come to assist. After three years, Agnes returned to Brooklyn and married Dr. Alfred Newhall, who joined in her work. His coming allowed a hospital to exist within the Home. By 1903, a second building was constructed which housed residents, the sick from the village, and ailing sailors from passing ships. "Mama and Papa Newhall" were beloved parents to many children until her death of a stroke in 1917. Five years later, he remarried to a staff member, Emma Supernaw.

A concert pianist, Simeon Oliver, and Gordon Gould, a founder of Alaska Pacific University in Anchorage, were both raised in the Home.

JESSE LEE HOME IN SEWARD

By 1925 the Methodists felt the Home could be run more economically and serve more Alaskans, if it were moved out of the Aleutians. Seward officials, eager to receive the Home, enticed the Methodists with (1) 100 acres of sloping hillside on the Seward Highway; (2) a more moderate climate reducing fuel costs; (3) and cheaper freight. The city would build a road to the property.

Dr. Newhall chose to assist the Presbyterians in Point Barrow. So the Rev. R.V.B Dunlap became the first of a long line of superintendents serving the Home in Seward. Among the children moving to Seward from Unalaska was Benny Benson. At age 13, and in the

7th grade, he entered a territory wide contest to design the Alaska flag. His winning flag flew for the first time on the grounds of the Home on July 9, 1927.

In 1942, World War II arrived in Alaska at Dutch Harbor in the Aleutians. Military installations were established at the entrance to Resurrection Bay near Seward. The Home was closed and the children relocated. A camouflage of evergreen trees was painted on the empty buildings. After the war, the Home was reopened and continued until the 1964 Alaska earthquake. No residents were injured, but the Girls Building became uninhabitable.

JESSE LEE HOME IN ANCHORAGE

With the Girls Building leveled, and social work moving toward foster homes to house needy children, the Home was receiving less residents. Anchorage needed an institution to serve mildly disturbed children, who were not seen as good candidates for foster care. So the Home redesigned its program and, using half of the $1,600,000 raised by U.S. Methodists churches for earthquake victims, built cottages on 25 acres in Anchorage. Since 1966 JLH has become a treatment center for children of physical abuse, neglect, or with behavioral problems. Rev. Richard Gilbert became the person who so ably conducted this transformation. The author served on its first board.

References for Preface

Arnett, Hans. Outline map of Alaska.

Boston University School of Theology: New England Conference Commission on Archives and History. Manuscript History collection.

Hays, Rev. Walter, Script for Slide Program, *The Jesse Lee Story.* Slide narration for slides *#27-28 and #38.*

Newhall, Edith Drugg, *"The Early History of the Jesse Lee Home,"* daughter of Dr. Albert and Agnes Newhall. This 1 1/2 page history was prepared and sent to the Rev. Walter Hays at his request on April 4, 1980.

Seward Phoenix Log, 12/5/25, pp. 4-5. Newspaper of Seward, Alaska. Prosperity Edition. Archives of the Seward Community Library. Research secured by Virginia Search Kirk in 1984.

Shepard, Bea & Claudia Kelsey, *HAVE GOSPEL TENT WILL TRAVEL.* The Methodist Church in Alaska since 1886. Copyright 1986 by Conference-Council on Ministries, Alaska Missionary Conference of the United Methodist Church, Anchorage, Alaska. References taken from pp. 19, 48, 127-129, and 144.

Woman's Home Missions, Volume 7, #12 1890. pp.181-182 by Mrs. L. Daggett.

INTRODUCTION

22 and the Mother of 11 is a story focusing on young women just out of college, and with no parenting skills, who commit to the roles of housemothers at the historical Jesse Lee Home in the 1950's in Seward, Alaska in 1952. The story depicts the challenges of being a parent figure for a dormitory of 10 or 11 children, who bring constant tattling, peer conflicts due to acts of mischief or relentless teasing, scratches/bruises, fractures, and an occasional temper tantrum. Clothing was always in need of repair, washing, and ironing. All of the children were in need of discipline, guidance and TLC.

In Book I of *22 and the Mother of 11*, Betty Jane and Dolores strive to provide all of the above, as they find themselves suddenly mothers and no longer college students. This story is based on the memoirs of their service from 1952-1954 . . . all before television, cell phones, and video games.

In order to protect the privacy of the children living within the walls of Jesse Lee Home in Seward in 1952-55, they have been given fictitious names in this writing. With few exceptions, real names are used for all adults in the book.

Chapter 1

BETTY JANE

The door opened from the interview room in the administration building on the Methodist campus of Scarritt College in Nashville. A young ministerial student stepped out with a frown on his face. The other missionary candidates gathered around him. "How was it?" asked one of them.

"They rejected me," he said in disgust.

"Why?" asked another one.

"They said my free thinking religious views might create unsettling situations."

I was listening intently to this conversation. *Oh dear! If they are going to ask me theology questions, I am doomed. Even I don't know what I think.*

"They suggested that I continue my studies in a theological seminary." With that said, he hastily grabbed his coat from the back of one of the chairs, and angrily left the building. The rest of the missionary candidates looked worried and fell silent.

Quickly I began to create some statement in my head about Jesus, God, and the Bible. On the bus coming over from Knoxville, no such thoughts had even entered my mind. After all, I was not going to preach. I wanted to work with war orphans in Korea. Already some of my friends were there fighting in the Korean War. My goal was to help the people of Korea, but not with guns *or* the Bible. But I did so want to say what this board wanted to hear.

Suddenly the door was opened again. A kindly, middle-aged woman stepped out and said, "Betty Jane Epps?" I stepped forward, "That's me." The lady smiled and said, "Step this way, Miss Epps."

Upon entering the room, I saw the committee of the National Mission Board of the Methodist Church sitting at tables in a U formation surrounding the candidate's chair. My eyes quickly scanned the mature faces of the men and women getting a first impression of Betty Jane Epps. The chairman of this powerful board introduced himself and then the others of his committee. He then invited me to sit in the empty chair and asked, "Why do you want to enter this short-term mission program?"

I breathed a sigh of relief. That question was easy. "I want to work with orphans. The Korean war is on and has taken several of my friends as soldiers, who speak of the orphans. I would like to work with war orphans, as my contribution to the war effort." My answer appeared acceptable. Friendly get-acquainted questions followed, creating a more relaxed atmosphere in the room. Finally they turned to the application itself.

"You have a very limited list of books you have read over the past year. Have you really read no more than this?"

My mind raced. *What kind of a question is this? Don't they realize I am a senior in college with a mountain of assignments every week? When do I have time for recreational reading? Is that important? Anyway in my few social hours, I want a date . . . not a book, but I'd better not tell them that.* Finally my memory banks produced the title of a book. "I don't believe the last book I read, other than college texts, is on my application. It was *The Greatest Story Ever Told* by Fulton Oursler." *That should impress her. It is the story of Jesus and a very thick book.*

The interviewer showed no signs of being impressed and condescendingly said, "I'm sure when school is out, your reading list will become longer and more varied."

"It would be nice to have more time for such," I politely added, hoping my response was what the interviewer wanted to hear.

Another woman spoke up. "Surely the Bible means more to you than a book of devotions." The interviewer smiled patronizingly. "I realize there isn't much space provided in which to write an answer. If you had more room would you add to this?"

It was obvious that this questioner thought my written view on what the Bible meant to me was a bit shallow and certainly less than profound. However, I knew that an honest answer would not have pleased this interviewer. Remembering the rejected ministerial student, I took evasive action. "Well, I certainly see the Bible as a guide for Christian living."

Preparing myself for rejection, I figured if that didn't suit this committee, I could always apply to the orphanage in Greenville, Tennessee. I would just give up on going to Korea. But suddenly I sensed that the third degree was over, for they began to talk about openings in both the Home and Foreign Mission programs that related to the needs of children

"We're sorry but the government will no longer allow us to send mission-aries into Korea. However, we do have an opening in our short-term mission program in Japan for settlement house work. The children are not orphans, but they do need a place for organized play and a nutritious meal."

From the other side of the U formation, another committee member spoke up. "If you would be willing to go to Alaska, we do have a children's institution there called Jesse Lee Home. It cares for Eskimo, Aleut, Indian, and Caucasian children, who can no longer live with their families. It is run by the Woman's Division of the Methodist Mission Board. We have two U.S.-2's there now and would like to send another. It is in a small town called Seward on the Kenai Peninsula in south central Alaska. However, we should tell you that the two in U.S.- 2 does not apply in the territories of our country or the foreign mission service. You would be expected to sign up for three years instead of two. It is only in the forty-eight states of the U.S. that you would serve for only two years. In other words, you'd be called a U.S-2, but your service would be for three years. Do you understand?"

"Yes, I do."

I could hardly believe my ears. *They must like me! They aren't offering one job but two!* It was a choice of Japan or Alaska. Finally the chairman concluded the interview by saying, "Why don't you consider the two offerings, and let us know in two weeks. At that point, we will make a final decision on your acceptance into the program."

It wasn't a tough decision. I wasn't good at foreign languages, and that would be an added burden in Japan. The Alaska offer was closer to my original intent. The climate was a consideration but obviously, other U.S.-2's were handling it, so why couldn't I? It was only for three years. By the time the Greyhound bus had pulled into Knoxville, my mind was made up.

It hadn't been a sure thing that my father would finance a college education. Four years previously, I had offered to work in his insurance office as his secretary, when not in classes, if he'd pay my tuition and books. Seventy-five dollars a quarter for tuition at the University of Tennessee would not have been an easy amount of money for him to come up with three times a year for four consecutive years. He made no commitment. He'd have to think about it.

My mother was working at the Fulton Sylphon Plant that made thermostats for heating units (among other things), and was excited that her daughter wanted to be a missionary. She could help some with the college expenses. She solicited the help of one of my brothers, who had gone to college on the GI bill after World War II. Morris convinced our father that it wasn't a waste of money to send a girl to college. "Even if the mission field doesn't work out for Betty, a college education is still beneficial," he declared to my Dad. My father did consent, and I studied diligently over the four years.

As graduation day drew near, I was still waiting for final confirmation from the Mission Board. When the letter came, I tore open the envelope and read aloud to my parents:

Dear Miss Epps:

This letter is to inform you that the advising medical officer recommends that the applicant not be accepted for missionary work in Alaska, until surgery is performed to remove a large cyst from an ovary. This decision is based on the fact that we do not know if medical facilities in 1952, in the territory of Alaska, are sophisticated enough for a major operation.

I stopped reading and looked at my parents. "I have a cyst?"

After a brief call to the doctor's office, we learned that I, indeed, had a cyst the size of a small grapefruit. It was a dilemma. How could I have this growth removed from an ovary with the usual six weeks recuperation period and finish up the final quarter of my senior year on the campus of the University of Tennessee? Why the training session for the U.S.-2's was to start in Kansas City, Missouri in June! Maybe this wasn't really necessary. "Let's get a second opinion," I said to my parents. "After all, I am in no pain, and there is no sign from the outside of my abdomen that something so large is growing inside." However, the first exam was confirmed, and the surgeon assured me if I entered the hospital after the ceremony on graduation day, I would miss only the first week of the six weeks training. That afternoon I wrote to the Department of Missions with the proposed date for surgery and permission to arrive a week late for training.

Recovering was uneventful, and within five weeks I was on a plane to Kansas City, Missouri. Training consisted of a bit of psychology, sociology, Methodist history, and Bible study. We grew as close as a family while eating, studying, worshiping, and playing together. One of the other U.S.-2's was a drama major, and led a small group of us to put on a play before the

The twenty-eight U.S.-2 Methodist short-term missionaries in the summer of 1952.
(Author is third from the left on the front row.)

staff and other trainees. I was given the role of an old woman living in Vermont; I'm sure my southern accent made me less than convincing, but we had fun. The end of the training came all too quickly for the camaraderie in this group of twenty-eight young people from Methodist churches all over the U.S. From Kansas City we would depart for work to many places throughout the U.S., including Hawaii and Alaska. Each agreed to write, but we knew eventually correspondence would wane, and slowly but surely, each personality would fade from our memories.

Although some of the U.S.'2's had to go directly to their assignments from the training center in Missouri, others were given an opportunity to return home to pack and say their goodbyes. Those final ten days included parties that gave me a royal send-off. The Methodist Woman's Society of Christian Service of the Knoxville District gave a city-wide luncheon in my honor and a gift of money to buy a warmer coat in Seattle. The event was published in one of the local newspapers, complete with picture. Even my father's fraternal insurance lodge gave a handkerchief shower. "What ever am I supposed to do with 30-40 hankies, Mom?" I laughed.

The author at a going away party.

"I don't know, but it was a loving, warm gesture from your father's lodge, and he appreciates this expression from them. You should too."

"Of course I do, Mama. But it's just not the sort of thing I would go out and buy for myself as preparation for living in Alaska."

"I know," she smiled. With a sigh she said, "You know I don't feel comfortable about airplanes. I don't understand what keeps them from falling out of the sky. Thank goodness you are going by ship at least part of the way. Why can't you go all the way to Seward by water from Seattle instead of flying? I'd certainly worry less about you."

"I guess they are short handed and are anxious for me to arrive as soon as possible. Going all the way by ship would take too long, so I'll have to fly from Juneau. I'll be alright, Mama." I handed her an envelope. "Here is the latest letter from Mr. Matthews, the superintendent of Jesse Lee Home."

Mama removed the letter from the envelope and began to read parts of the letter aloud.

"Your coming will make the staff at Jesse Lee Home complete for the first time in years. We are anxious to have you arrive."

"So you see, Mama, if it hadn't been for Miss Burris, I probably would be flying all the way."

"Miss Burris?" she asked.

"Miss Burris is the official from the Woman's Division of the Mission Board, who visited the U.S.-2's at the training center. She told us that she had just returned from a trip to Alaska going by Alaska Steamship up the inside passage. She raved about that trip to me! Wanted me to have the same experience! I'm lucky."

"You sure are!" commented my Dad, as he walked into the room carrying a large black trunk trimmed in metal. "Your mother says we should let you have this old trunk to pack all your stuff in. What do you think?"

"We can ship it ahead, can't we? I don't want to carry that big thing with me."

"You fill it, and I'll take care of the rest. I'll take it to the post office."

"Thanks, Dad."

"Yep, I looked that trip up on the map. That inside passage is along the southeastern panhandle of Alaska. If I could afford it, I'd go with you. What an adventure that must be to ride on a big ship."

"Miss Burris said that it's a travel experience unequaled. 'You must have it!' she told me. She even apologized that she has to take me off of the ship at Juneau, but I'll have a day or two to visit there. It's the capitol, you know."

"Yessiree, you're lucky, young lady."

"Well, I've never been on a big plane like she's going on, but that don't make me want to go with her. I'll be prayin' for you all the way," said Mama worriedly. Mama had always been a worrier, and there was nothing to be done about that. "Now, Betty, if you run into problems anywhere along the way, find yourself a Methodist Church, and those people will help you. If you'll do that, I won't worry about you."

"Now, Mama, I'll be okay. I have the name of the hotel in Seattle. I will simply take a taxi from the airport. But I'll remember your advice, if I need it." So I patted her reassuringly on the shoulder.

On the day I was to leave, all of the relatives who could get away during the middle of the day came to see me off. It was a big occasion for the family. I was doing something special. In 1952 flying in an airplane was a dress-up occasion. There were no blue jeans in sight, and most of the male travelers wore ties and coats. I was wearing a new suit and a brown velvet hat with a veil and, of course, dress gloves. I had on new brown suede toeless high heels and felt more like a fashion model than a missionary. As I boarded the plane and saw the attire of my fellow travelers, I knew I had made the correct wardrobe choice. It was dark when we reached Seattle, and the gorgeous array of electrical lights spread for miles under the huge plane. It was like a miniature city laid out on a huge table beneath us! The sight almost took my breath away. Tiny cars and trucks were moving along the thoroughfares lined with small trees. As we came in for a landing, I found it almost disappointing to see everything grow to normal size.

After picking up my luggage, I took a taxi to the hotel the Mission Board had chosen. It had a huge lobby and looked very elegant. I felt very lucky indeed to be receiving such treatment. However, I was in for a rude awakening when the young hotel clerk informed me that he had no reservation for a Betty Jane Epps. "Oh, but you must! Look again. I didn't make the reservation. It was made by the Methodist Mission Board in New York City. You *must* have me down."

The author with parents, Gale and Mildred Epps, at the Tyson McGhee Airport in Knoxville, Tennessee, as she was leaving for Alaska.

"Do you have a receipt or any confirmation that the reservation was made?"

I quickly went through all of the papers that the Mission Board had sent. Finally I found the name of the hotel typed on the itinerary. That was all.

"Sorry. There has been a probable break down in communication, but we simply do not have a room for you. The entire hotel is booked for a convention and unfortunately, because of the convention, most of the downtown hotels are full."

I felt panic. It was very late at night, and I hadn't the slightest idea how to go about finding another hotel in this unfamiliar city. The fact was I had never made a hotel reservation in my life. Ahhh, the Methodist Church. Could I take my mother's advice? No. No Methodist minister would be up at this hour. Bewildered, I said to the desk clerk, "I've never been to Seattle. How do I find another hotel? And what can I do with these bags?"

"Well, you can leave your bags here while you look. How many nights are you staying in Seattle?"

"Only one. Tomorrow afternoon I board an Alaska Steamship for Alaska. Don't you have just one room for just this night?"

"No, not in this hotel." The hotel clerk quickly analyzed the pleading young image before him. Was he looking at a small town girl frightened by the insensitive and uncaring ways of the big city? What could he do? Suddenly he had a solution. "But wait a minute. If you don't mind staying in a small hotel, maybe I can help you."

"Oh, I don't mind! By all means, do whatever you can." He left momentarily. I used that time as constructively as I knew how. I prayed hard and fast. Within a few minutes he was back.

"Now, it's an old hotel but it's clean, and they have one room available. My cousin manages it. It is only a few blocks away. I'll have one of our bellhops walk over with you to carry your bags."

I felt I could have kissed him, but instead, broke into all smiles and thanked him profusely. The bellhop chose the back alley as a short-cut, but somehow I felt safe with him. The contrast in size of the two hotels stunned me. The lobby of this new hotel was no bigger than an entryway. Second thoughts ran through my head, but did I have a choice? A very handsome man probably in his thirties greeted me and apologized that there would be a short wait, while his wife made up the room. He explained that their establishment was a boarding hotel with kitchen privileges, and they were giving me a one-room-efficiency for the night. He filled the time with talk of places to see in Seattle. I explained that I would have only the next morning and would need to check in at the Alaska Steamship office concerning my reservation.

A telephone call indicated that the room was ready. We took an aging elevator that looked like a wrought iron cage and made our way to an upper floor. The room was very small and I saw no bed.

"Where is the bed?"

"Right over here in the wall." I had heard about such things but had never seen one. He quickly opened the doors of what looked like a closet, and presto, a bed came down fully made and ready for sleeping. "Shall I leave it down?" he asked.

"Yes, thank you." I gave him the amount of money my father had advised was appropriate for a tip. I hoped a dollar would be sufficient. He smiled and left me alone. The room smelled of age but it was clean, and at last I had a bed, and my problems were over for the night. My final thought before laying my head on the soft pillow was to never again take prearranged travel arrangements for granted.

The next morning I made a phone call from my room to the Alaska Steamship Line and was relieved to learn that they did, indeed, have a reservation for Betty Jane Epps on the *Aleutian*. Now I was free to shop for the coat. The handsome man at the desk smiled a warm greeting, as I stepped out of the noisy, quaint, little elevator.

"And which of the morning tours have you chosen to see our beautiful city?"

"I'm afraid that will have to wait until next time. This morning I must shop for a coat to keep me warm in Alaska. Are there department stores near by?"

"Ahhh, Alaska! You want a fur coat?"

"No, I don't have enough money for that. Do you think I can survive without one?"

"How long are you going to stay in Alaska?"

"Three years."

He laughed. "Oh, I don't know. Alaska is pretty cold." He added flirtatiously, "Maybe you should change your mind and stay with us in Seattle. Then you won't need a fur coat."

"Really? It's hard to imagine a state this far north where one doesn't need a fur coat?"

He broke into a smile and showed brilliant white teeth, accented by a well-coifed dark moustache. "Well, we have the warm Japanese current that keeps us cozy all winter. And if you stay," he added with a twinkle in his eye, "we will keep you cozy too."

The warm Japanese current . . . hadn't I seen that somewhere on a geography test? It was strange to hear it discussed outside of the academic classroom.

"How about it? Will you stay with us?" he asked, as he reached for something above his head. "Or are you going to insist that I give you this map of our city marked with all of the large department stores within walking distance?"

"I must insist on the map. I have a job waiting for me in Alaska. I'll be checking out after lunch."

He left his desk to open the door for me. "I wouldn't want you to think that Seattle men are not gentlemen."

And somewhat flirtatious . . . I thought but yet flattered by the attention of an older man. I walked up the street in the direction of the shopping area feeling just a tiny bit evil. A married man had flirted with me and, yes, I had enjoyed it. Oh, dear, are young missionaries allowed that pleasure?

Chapter 2

"BETTY JANE—BUDDING ROMANCES GO AWRY

Buying a coat was always a major project in my family. Coats were expensive and thus merited careful selection. I had never had to make this decision alone. The salesladies were no help. They marveled over every style I tried on. Finally I explained, "I need something very warm because I am moving to Alaska." My statement was like electricity. Suddenly the whole floor buzzed. I was surrounded by clerks hoping to get a look at this adventurous girl willing to live in Alaska. Their reaction was surprising. Surely would-be Alaskan residents came through Seattle all the time. Well, several had heard of an occasional friend of an acquaintance who had gone up maybe for the summer, or perhaps some relative had to go there because of the military, but no, they hadn't known many people who were willing to go up there and *live* . . . three years. Finally, a dress coat in colorful rust with a raised collar (to keep the wind out) and a new lightweight lining seemed just the choice to keep me very warm. The sleeves fit snugly at the wrists (another *must* as the Alaskan winds would surely freeze my arms). The coat was $55.00. I had more than enough money to pay for it. The Knoxville Methodist women had given me $50.00 and my parents had given another $25.00 (assuming warmer coats cost more). I wasn't sure it was the right coat, but much time had elapsed and I had to make a decision. Well, it was heavier than the green gabardine coat left behind in Tennessee. Perhaps it would do.

The taxi driver had obviously carried many steamship passengers to the docks, as he knew exactly where to check bags. It was quite a relief to hear the baggage man repeat my name from his printed list of reservations. "Go ahead and get on board, Miss. Your bags will soon be in your room." Looking up at the people standing on the decks of the *Aleutian*, I scanned the scene quickly in search of friendly faces. Lively, happy music was coming from the loud speakers on board the ship creating a festive atmosphere in the expressions on the faces of the passengers. As we say in Tennessee, "This ain't gonna be nothin' but fun!" With that reassuring thought, I moved quickly up the gangplank, knowing full well that I was being scrutinized by a bevy of curious beings above. It was okay. I was just as curious about them. *Who knows? Perhaps one of them will provide me with an exciting experience I will recall in years to come.* Once on board the *Aleutian*, I stood in line at the purser's office to get a cabin assignment. I was surrounded by people middle-aged and older, who were commenting to each other about this being the last voyage of the *Aleutian* to Alaska. I kept glancing over my shoulder hoping someone in my own age range would come into view. It didn't happen. The purser was especially friendly and asked if my destination was Juneau.

"No, my destination is Seward, but I'm getting off in Juneau."

"How long will you be in Seward?"

"Three years."

"Oh, you'll love it. Here is your table assignment, and this will be your seating for each meal. Any questions?"

"Just one. How do I find my cabin?" As he gave me directions, I observed that this tall, blonde, Scandinavian type was on the edge of middle-age himself. The attractive uniform, warm smile, and curly hair had no doubt dazzled many a young woman in the past.

I found the cabin with no problem and was surprised by the small size of the compartment. As the baggage man had predicted, there sat the bags. They took up most of the floor space. Obviously, the cabins on this deck were designed just for sleeping.

After dinner I took a walk on the decks to familiarize myself with this new floating home. Obviously, many passengers were doing the same. On one of the higher decks, I found a place by the rails and watched the water swiftly flow away from the moving ship. Occasional lights could be seen along the Canadian coastline. As I turned to investigate another part of the ship, a young woman greeted me. She was accompanied by two young sailors.

"Hi! We're looking for people our age, and you seem to be about it. Would you like to join us?" she asked.

Were they ever a sight for sore eyes! Introductions were made, and they told me they were Coast Guard employees enroute to their assignment in Ketchikan, Alaska. One of the sailors was married to the young woman. The other sailor remarked, "We saw you come aboard and looked for you in the dining room. Where were you sitting?" Apparently I had been assigned a different hour.

"We'll get that changed," said the young woman.

"Do you think the purser would change it?" I eagerly replied.

"Sure he will," her husband insisted. "Tomorrow we'll all go to see him . . . right after breakfast."

The next morning they caught me as I was exiting the dining room from breakfast. "We did it! We fixed it! The purser didn't mind at all." I was relieved. From that point on, the Coast Guard and I were inseparable. We played cards; we danced; we sang; we laughed and yes, the unattached sailor and I even romanced. We seemed to lose track of time as we strolled the decks in the moonlight, long after the other passengers had retired. As Ketchikan was the first stop on the route north, we knew that the time was short. The married couple began to give us more time alone, sensing that something was growing between us.

"I thought you were a ballerina when I first saw you coming up the gang plank. I would never have guessed that you are a missionary." I blushed, accepting this as a compliment. "Hey, sometimes the Guard makes trips to Seward. I'll try and pull that duty. Then we can see each other again."

"Please do! I'd like that very much. Promise me you'll try."

"I will," he said looking lovingly into my eyes. Suddenly he was kissing me like I had never been kissed before. If this was love, I was in it. He became more passionate in his wooing, and it soon became a monumental effort to resist him. Mixed emotions welled up inside of me. However, my head kept a stern hand over the desires of my body.

You idiot! You can't fall in love with this guy. It's illogical. You're a missionary about to start a three-year term. You may never see him again. Reason with him. Such thoughts were flooding my head, but he was in no mood for reasoning, and Mother Nature's feet seemed firmly planted in his camp. With the moon shining on quiet waters rippling behind the stern of the ship, no evening setting was ever more romantic. We were bewitched . . . both of us.

"I have to ask you something," he said softly. "At first I thought you knew, but now I'm convinced that you've never known."

"Known what?" I asked.

"Did you notice on the day we first met that I was wearing a wedding ring?"

"No!" I was shocked. "Are you trying to tell me you're married?"

"Yes, but my wife and I are thinking about getting a divorce."

My heart sank. "Where is your ring now? Why aren't you wearing it?"

"It's back in the cabin. I took it off the next morning. I wasn't sure you knew. We were having so much fun together, I was afraid it would make a difference with you. Does it?"

Still stunned, I said, "I had no idea you were married!" Then I looked straight into that handsome, deceitful face that now framed apologetic eyes and said, "You know it makes a difference. Where I come from this is all wrong."

"I'm sorry. But my marriage is breaking up. I thought that made it okay."

"But you're still married. You should have told me!" Thoughts in my head kept screaming, this is definitely behavior unbecoming to a missionary! He took me in his arms and held me close not saying a word. Finally he spoke, "How do you feel now?"

"I'm sorry but I feel . . . awful." I pushed him away. "I have to go to my cabin."

"Will I see you at breakfast?"

"Yes. Sure." I walked back to the cabin filled with guilt and love for a married man. I spent a restless night chiding myself for not being more observing of his left hand. If he was truly getting a divorce, did that make it less wrong? My conscience wasn't so sure, so we did battle most of the night.

By breakfast time I had concluded that within a few hours these three people would probably be walking out of my life forever, and nothing was to be gained to part on less than friendly terms. And so, they departed the ship.

In comparison, the rest of the trip was subdued. Yes, it was beautiful to be for sure, but the excitement was gone. The waiter sensed my feeling and tried to be entertaining. "You're being very nice to me but really, I'm embarrassed to be the single diner at this large table. I'll ask the purser to place me elsewhere, so I'll have some people to talk to."

Much to my surprise, the waiter responded with something akin to desperation. "Oh, no! Don't do that! I'll talk to you. Why I'll even do a tap dance if you'll stay. You won't be bored. I promise."

"Forget it," I laughed. "I won't make you dance."

"But I love to dance, and I'm good. You'll enjoy it." His persistence puzzled me. "Just give me one more meal. If the entertainment is not equal to your enjoyment of the elegant food, I'll let you move to another waiter's table. It will make me sad, but I'll do it."

I smiled, "Okay, one more meal." I had to admit that at the next meal, he was very amusing, and his dedication to serve only me was flattering. He never left me alone, except to bring in another course or return used dishes to the kitchen.

"There now! You weren't bored were you? And I even had you laughing. Now, will you stay at my table?"

"You certainly lived up to your word. But if I move, don't you see I'll be doing you a favor? You won't have to work, unless you assist at one of the other tables."

"No, you don't understand. Each of us is assigned a separate table." He looked at me sadly, "I don't draw waiter's wages if my table is empty."

So that was it. He had tried amusement, flattery, guilt, and now sympathy, all to increase his earnings. If I left him, I would definitely be playing the heavy, so I stayed; allowing this middle-aged man to fill my head with stories of his life, Alaska, and the *Aleutian,* all the way to Juneau. He was indeed an interesting character, and I was certainly never bored.

The ship passed Wrangell, and shortly afterward, Petersburg. Both were tiny fishing communities. The *Aleutian* dropped anchor only briefly. We were told that only Scandinavians were welcome to live in Petersburg.

On the trip up to Juneau, I dropped by the purser's office. "So there you are. I've been wondering about you," was his happy greeting.

"I just want to say thanks for all your help. I have really enjoyed this trip. I'm getting off in Juneau tomorrow, you know."

"Yes, I know, but have I asked you why you can't stay on and go all the way to Seward with us?" I explained that I was needed at my job right away.

"Well, you've had the best of the trip. Once we leave the inside passage along the coast and get into open water in the Pacific, it gets rough sometimes."

"You mean like seasick?"

"Some do, if it gets real rough."

"I don't think I'd enjoy that."

"Well, you'll enjoy Juneau. It's a pretty place. Small, but it's the capitol, you know."

"What should I see my two days there?"

"Let me think . . . the territorial legislature isn't in session, but if you're interested in government, you can easily see the legislative buildings, and of course, the governor's mansion by just walking around. Then take a tour bus to see the Mendenhall Glacier. That's a must. Most want to see the Red Dog Saloon, but be careful, it gets pretty rowdy. It's right down town."

"Thanks. I'll take your advice and walk on by."

"You know, now and then we get passengers interested in visiting Jesse Lee Home. I may surprise you sometime and bring some up. Would you give us a tour?"

"Sure. By then I will have learned the ropes."

"Spoken like a true sailor. Good luck to you."

"Thanks . . . and the same to you."

Like Ketchikan, Juneau was tucked into the side of a mountain and thus, hilly. It was very picturesque, but it appeared to have limited land for expansion due to the steep cliffs. I saw very little construction on the mountains, as everything was located near the base of this steep terrain. I easily found the government buildings and the governor's mansion. The residence was built, surprisingly, in southern architecture with white pillars. Even if there were no signs, no one could mistake it for any thing but the home of the governor. As I walked down the steep hill back into the business district, I noticed a church-like structure built right up to the edge of the sidewalk. Land appeared to be at a premium in this town, and no church could likely afford the luxury of spacious lawns, so commonly found around churches in the South. The glass encased sign read, "First Methodist Church of Juneau, Rev. Fred McGinnis, Minister." My curiosity was piqued, and immediately I felt as though I was in the presence of an old friend, even though it came in the form of a structure instead of a human. I slowly opened the door and stepped inside. Since this was not a Sunday, the sanctuary was empty. It was as though I had been there before. There is a certain sameness in the worship areas of all Methodist churches. Is it because they all order their accessories from the lone Methodist Publishing House in Nashville? At any rate, that sameness gave comfort and reassurance to this young woman thousands of miles from home. I heard the tapping of typewriter keys. *That must be the pastor's study.* My feet followed the sound that led down the aisle and past the altar to a small office located behind the front of the sanctuary. An attractive, dark haired man got to his feet as soon as he saw me come into view.

"Hello. My name is Betty Epps, and I am a short-term missionary enroute to Seward, Alaska to work at the Jesse Lee Home. The church door was open, so I just walked in."

"I'm happy to meet you," he said warmly. "Do sit down." My feet were very grateful for that invitation. I had been climbing the Juneau hills in high heeled dress shoes. Rev. McGinnis had heard of the U.S.-2 program and seemed quite interested. Before I left, the minister told me that his younger brother was working in Juneau and living at the parsonage. Then the Reverend asked if I would care to join the family for dinner that evening. I was delighted to have the invitation and received directions to the parsonage only a few steps away.

If the rest of the family is as nice as this man, I am in for an enjoyable evening, I thought, as I concluded the walking tour and entered the Baranof Hotel. The desk clerk handed me an envelope and said that it had been delivered to the hotel in the afternoon. "Who could be writing to me? The only person I know in Juneau, I just left only five minutes ago."

"I believe it is from the Alaska steamship *Aleutian*, ma'am. The stationery indicates so." I was puzzled even more. There was no name in the upper left hand corner for a return address . . . just my name on the front of the envelope in very legible writing.

Climbing the hills had taken its toll in my uterus. I felt a severe case of cramps coming on. "Does the hotel have a hot water bottle? I'm not feeling well. I'm going to need one very shortly."

"We'll send one up right away, ma'am."

"Thank you."

I sighed with relief as I sat on the bed and kicked off my shoes. The cramping was beginning to increase. I lay down hoping it would pass. I opened the mystery letter from the ship. To my amazement, it was a love letter extolling my physical beauty; and by the third paragraph, it was a *proposal of marriage*.

*"I know that the fun we had on board in our conversations mean that we are very compatible and certainly above letting the color differences in our skin stand in the way of the great love we hold for each other. Will you marry me? If so, we can do the ceremony in Seward when the **Aleutian** docks."*

Having been raised in the South, my segregated existence produced a naiveté that carried the social garbage of the early 1950's, and my conservative mind, at the time, went into shock. Thoughts raced through my brain reliving those dining room conversations, trying to uncover anything I might have said to this middle-aged waiter to encourage such action. Nothing. The absurdity of it all seemed to increase the cramping in my abdomen. I rang the desk. "Would you please send up the hot water bottle I requested?" It was a new voice, ignorant of the original request, but assured me the bottle would be up soon.

My mind began to perceive negative scenes of this unexpected suitor pursuing me in Seward. I hadn't even reached my destination, and already a Coast Guardsman had turned me into a Jezebel, and a man near twice my age is asking me to enter into an interracial marriage. *Is this par for the course for young missionaries enroute to mission posts in Alaska? How am I to explain this crazy situation to my new employer and fellow workers? Surely their imaginations will run wild, when this waiter from the ship appears on our door step demanding my hand in marriage. Now I am frightened. Obviously, he is unpredictable.* By now the contractions in my uterus are unbearable. "If you can't get me a hot water bottle, then you'll have to get me a doctor!" I demanded of the Desk a third time.

"What's wrong, ma'am?"

"I have stomach cramps."

"Oh, I'm sorry you are ill. You see the delay is that we don't have a hot water bottle in the hotel, but I have just sent the bellhop out to buy one. You should have it in less than ten minutes." I managed to moan a thank you.

The heat from the hot water bottle dulled the pain enough for me to fall into a light sleep. When I awoke, the time on the clock indicated it was time for me to prepare for the dinner engagement. But one movement of my body and I knew it was no use. I would have to call and cancel. I reached for the telephone. A pleasant female voice answered. That was a relief. It would be easier to explain my predicament to a woman. Mrs. McGinnis was very understanding and knew that I would feel better the next day. Being a gracious hostess, she insisted that I come the next night. I accepted.

Harriet McGinnis was right. I felt much better upon awakening the next morning. I took a late breakfast and a brief walk limiting my tour to the area around the Baranof. Within moments, the renowned Red Dog Saloon came into view. I was yet to learn that most towns and cities in Alaska had at least one drinking establishment that was more notorious than the rest, with any number of questionable activities taking place.

Like the church, this structure also sprang straight up at the edge of the sidewalk. The rough wooden boards concealed any activity that was going on inside. I slowed my pace to take in this establishment with such an illustrious reputation. Simultaneously the door opened, and a strong smell of beer and the loud sound of music from a probable jukebox flooded my senses. I was tempted to go in and satisfy my curiosity. However, my better judgment warned me that visiting the minister's home and this saloon all in the same day might appear incongruous for a young lady entering the mission field. Suddenly my sensitive uterus reminded me that it was time to return to the hotel and rest up for the social event of the evening.

Harriet McGinnis was every bit as warm and hospitable as her husband had been the day before. She was a slender, attractive woman with bright sparkling eyes and a smile that immediately put one at ease. I was introduced to the youngest member of the family, a brown-eyed, precocious preschooler with a tooth missing in the front. He was full of personality and challenged his father for center ring until finally, Harriet brought the game to a halt and put Timmy to bed. They apologized for the absence of the minister's brother saying, "Although he was free the night before, he has a conflict this evening. We're so sorry. We wanted him to meet you."

"I'm sorry too. I would have liked to have met him." That wasn't just a polite remark. I was banking on the brother having just half the charm of the minister. If so, I knew I would have been in for a memorable evening. As we sat down to dinner, they wanted to know how much of Juneau I had been able to see and specifically, if I had seen the Mendenhall Glacier. "I had hoped to take a tour bus there yesterday but when I grew ill, I went to bed instead."

"When does your plane leave tomorrow morning?"

I told him.

"Good. We'll pick you up and give you a quick tour of the glacier. It's on the way." Naturally I was delighted. Before the evening was over, we were on a first name basis, and I had received all the information Fred and Harriet McGinnis knew about the present life of the Jesse Lee Home. I decided to tell them about the love letter from the *Aleutian* waiter and asked Fred's advice on how to deal with the situation. He advised me to leave it in the hands of Mr. Matthews, the Jesse Lee Home superintendent, and let him turn the waiter away at the door. It seemed a logical action.

"I think I'm going to tell her, Fred. It will serve you right for trying to play a joke on me." Harriet was grinning from ear to ear.

"You're going to enjoy this, Harriet. I don't think I can stop you."

She threw back her head and laughed; then gently placed her hand on his. "You don't mind, do you, dear?"

"No. Go ahead. Perhaps she'll enjoy it."

"Yesterday I received this call from Fred saying that he had just met this delightful, little old woman, who was on her way to work at Jesse Lee Home. 'She is so old,' he said, 'I'm surprised that the Mission Board is considering using her. My heart just went out to her, Harriet. I lost my head and invited her for dinner tonight. Is that all right?' "

I glanced at Fred, who was obviously pleased with the progress of his little joke at this point.

"I assured him that it was all right and told Fred's brother we would be having company for dinner. I didn't give it another thought until your call came yesterday saying you were sick. If I sounded a bit puzzled, it's because your youthful voice didn't fit into the picture that Fred had prepared for me. After informing him that you called to cancel but would be coming tomorrow night I added, 'Why, Fred, she didn't sound old at all.' For a moment he looked like the cat that had swallowed the canary but quickly recovered and said, 'Oh, but wait until you see her.' She laughed again. "Well, I have seen you, and you don't fit the picture at all."

I smiled but my eyes were questioning his motivation.

"I suppose this requires some explanation," he offered. "You see my brother has been complaining about the lack of social life in Juneau. He says the women are too young or else too old. When I met you yesterday, I was so impressed with your youth, your charm, and your attractiveness, that I seized the opportunity to make you a surprise package for my brother. Also I knew that Harriet would enjoy your company. I figured I could get by with fabricating old age, as most people envisage the typical children's home worker at least middle-age and many in the older age bracket. Obviously, you don't fit that image, and I was so looking forward to seeing expressions on the faces of both my wife and my younger brother, when you came through the door. Unfortunately, I was too convincing. My brother told Harriet he didn't feel up to trying to make conversation with an old woman. He thought he'd take in an early movie and have a hamburger down town."

I had to laugh. Although his practical joke robbed me of meeting the brother, it really was funny . . . and flattering.

The next day the view of the magnificent glacier was breath taking. It was exciting to see ice now floating as icebergs, after having been locked into the body of this massive river of ice for probably thousands of years. How many people get such an opportunity? This spectacular scene made me realize why my host and hostess insisted that no one should be allowed to leave Juneau without seeing the Mendenhall Glacier. I said good-bye to my new friends and boarded the plane for Anchorage, where I would spend the night in the Anchorage Hotel. The following day I would fly into Seward in a smaller plane and begin life as a U.S.-2.

Chapter 3

DOLORES ARRIVES

A thin man of medium height and his wife of similar size began to eye each of the female passengers stepping off the train from Anchorage. They heard the conductor give a parting farewell to each passenger. When Dolores Morey appeared he exclaimed, "Well, here you are young lady. Welcome to Seward, Alaska."

"Do you see Elwin Matthews anywhere?" Dolores quickly inquired of the conductor.

Sensing someone approaching him from the rear, the conductor turned and said, "Why here he is now, the Superintendent of Jesse Lee Home! Hello, Mr. Matthews."

Elwin Matthews was hoping that the young woman with the conductor was his new staff member. "Dolores Morey, I presume?" She answered yes. "We're happy you have arrived. Thank you, Mr. Milroy, for bringing my summer staff member safely to Seward. I see you have met her."

"That I have. I can tell you anything you want to know."

"Uh oh," said Dolores.

"Don't worry, I won't tell him everything,"

"Whew!" said Dolores going along with the charade. "I discovered the conductor knows my father's family back in Quilcene, Washington. So he could very well pull some skeletons out of the closet that even I don't know about."

"That righhhhhht?" smiled Mr. Matthews in a Texas drawl.

"Oh, you wouldn't do that to her would you, Mr. Milroy?" asked Ruth Matthews, joining the group.

"Her secrets are safe with me on one condition . . . that you let me come out to Jesse Lee sometime, so this young lady can bring me up to date on her family."

"I think that can be arranged," said Mr. Matthews. "By the way," he turned to Dolores, "this is my wife, Ruth." A warm greeting was exchanged by the two women.

"We'll pick up your bags and then drive out to Jesse Lee," said Mr. Matthews leading the way to the baggage area.

"We trust you haven't had dinner," stated Ruth.

"No food on that train," replied Dolores.

"Dinner has already been served in our dining room, but we brought plates of food over to our house. We'll heat it up for you, but Elwin and I have already eaten."

"That's very thoughtful of you. Thank you," said Dolores

Dolores quickly spotted her bags, and the three carried them to the car. Mr. Matthews drove along the water's edge saying, "This body of water is called Resurrection Bay, and we have a nice view of the Bay from Jesse Lee Home."

Mr. Matthews turned the car northward away from the bay and headed up a graveled road that led to the business area of Seward. No pavement was in sight, as they moved through the two or three blocks of downtown Seward.

"You've just seen the shopping area of Seward," stated Ruth.

"Not much, is there?" remarked Dolores.

"No, just the essentials . . . couple of clothing stores, a grocery store, the bank, a few tourist shops, and the post office a block over. Well, there are a few eating places and a small bakery, a movie theatre, and several churches, plus liquor establishments," replied Ruth.

"No hospital?" asked Dolores.

"Yes, that's a block over towards the mountains. It's small but Seward's population is under three thousand," added Elwin.

"We do have a tuberculosis sanatorium out near us for mostly natives. It too is run by the Methodists. Some of the parents of our children are patients there," added Ruth.

"Do they ever get to see them?"

"Yes, when the Sanatorium feels the patients are well enough to have us bring over a family of children. The patients are usually masked, but the kids are used to seeing their parents that way," said Ruth.

Within a short time the passengers in the car began to feel the effects of a very bumpy road. "Sorry about that," said Mr. Matthews. "We're on the lagoon road. It's always full of potholes." Dolores looked out of the car windows and observed that the road had been built between two bodies of water.

The bumpy, unpaved lagoon road in 1952 in Seward, Alaska.

"Especially after a rain," added Ruth. "The road doesn't get graded as often as we'd like. We may notice it more than others with our school bus going back and forth from town four times a day. Not to mention all of the trips the Jesse Lee Home pickup truck makes daily to the post office and often to the docks to pick up supplies."

"Why does the bus go four times a day?" inquired Dolores.

"You see, we bring the big kids home for lunch. It's cheaper and less labor intensive than trying to pack that many lunches five days a week. They attend the high school in town, and we take them back for afternoon classes. The little ones walk back and forth to Bayview School behind Jesse Lee."

"How many people live at Jesse Lee Home now?"

"Counting staff, around one hundred," responded Mr. Matthews. The car turned to the left towards the mountains and then north on a straight road passing empty fields and meadows, where a few cows were grazing.

"Do those cows belong to Jesse Lee Home?" asked Dolores.

"No," said Ruth. "They belong to the Seward Dairy. I believe the Dairy just leases this land for grazing. Up ahead you can see the buildings that make up Jesse Lee Home." Three large buildings came into view, each connected by a smaller structure called an arcade attaching one building to the other. The large buildings appeared to be three stories high with windows all around. A large stretch of empty land covered with wild grass and rocks extended in front of the three buildings. Two short and wide concrete posts with the words "Jesse Lee Home" on one and "1925" on the other announced that they were entering this property.

"Do the buildings have trees painted on them?" asked Dolores in surprise.

Camouflage of trees painted on Jesse Lee Home building that housed the dining area. Photo from Mrs. George Green's collection.

"Yes, that's camouflage put on during World War II," offered Mr. Matthews.

"It's 1952 and it's still there?!" exclaimed Dolores.

The residence of the superintendent of Jesse Lee Home, Seward, Alaska and two concrete posts announcing the entrance to the JLH grounds. One bears the name of the Home and the other, 1925, the year the Home was moved from the Aleutians to Seward. Photo from Rachel Yokel's collection.

"I'm afraid so but we've applied for funds to paint the buildings," he replied.

"Over to the right, you'll see a white cottage facing the mountains and the three main buildings. That's the superintendent's residence. We live there with our two boys," said Ruth, as the car drove past the front of the institution's middle building and then turned right past the next one.

Mr. Matthews parked the car to the right of the white cottage, and Dolores followed the Matthews up the few concrete steps to the front door. Once inside the house, Ruth scurried around in the kitchen warming the food mentioned earlier at the railroad station. Mr. Matthews showed Dolores the bathroom and the living room and offered to let her freshen up before eating. As they waited in the comfortable chairs in the living room, Mr. Matthews began to talk about a typical day at Jesse Lee Home.

"Are there any specific do's and don'ts that house parents need to be aware of before I make any giant boo-boos?" asked Dolores.

"Well, at the table we try to set the example by eating all of whatever is put on our plates . . . with a smile. You'll find the kids are pretty good eaters, but occasionally, something will be placed in front of them that may cause a complaint."

"Can't make any faces, huh?" laughed Dolores. "What about allergies? Any problem with food allergies here?"

"The Woman's Division has hired a dietician, who decides the menu for both the Home and the San. That was one of the dietician's first questions, but there has been no problem yet. So no, we don't allow the kids to plead an allergy to something that they do not want to eat. Actually, Helen is very good. She has tried to broaden their tastes by varying the menu. Has even introduced Texas pinto beans to the kids, and I liiiiiiiike those," he said with a big Texas smile. "Tonight was liver and onions. Most had never had that before."

Suddenly Dolores silently panicked, *Oh no! Liver and onions! That is not my favorite food. Do please let it be a small piece.*

Ruth called from the kitchen, "Dinner is ready!"

"Thank you!" said Dolores politely. Oh well, maybe the vegetable will be something I like, she thought. Mr. Matthews led the young woman into the dining room. Once they sat down at the table, Ruth brought in a plate with two slices of warmed over liver and onions, warmed over canned peas, and a plain green gelatin salad on the side. Not canned peas! thought Dolores. *Well, when in Rome, do as the Romans do,* she silently sighed and began to use a sawing motion to cut through the tough meat that had lost a lot of its moisture in the reheating. Unfortunately, in 1952, microwave ovens, that would quickly heat food and give it less of a leftover taste, were yet to come.

"Yes," said Ruth, "Helen Priebe insists that nutrition is always uppermost in her planning. We are lucky to have her come up from Texas to join us." Dolores attempted polite conversation, in spite of this horrible feeling of captivity in the food choices of the trained dietician. Could she handle this for three whole months? What had she gotten herself into?

After dinner Ruth and Elwin Matthews led Dolores on a tour of the Jesse Lee Home, beginning with the residence for the boys, the building closest to the nearby mountains. As they moved quickly through the halls, Dolores observed both dark haired and light haired children in pajamas carrying toothbrushes back and forth from bathrooms to their respective dormitory rooms, and each looking curiously at the newcomer. Greetings were spontaneously given to Mr. and Mrs. Matthews. As they came upon a house parent, the new staff member was introduced. Climbing the stairs to the three floors, Dolores observed that the youngest boys were housed on the first floor, while the oldest boys were on the top. This was also true in the residence for the girls, except no girls were living on the third floor. Instead, this area was used for storage for mostly new and used clothing for both the boys and the girls. They passed through the arcades from one building to the next with the large dining room in the middle building. There was no activity in the kitchen that adjoined the spacious dining room. Ruth commented that Marge Echols, the cook, had probably long since retired to her apartment on the second floor with her husband, Peter, one of the maintenance men.

"They have a young son, Malvin, age eleven or twelve, who lives there with them. You'll meet them at breakfast in the morning," said Mr. Matthews.

Dolores followed Ruth up a narrow flight of stairs and was soon standing in the large library situated across from the cook's apartment. "The older children come here to do their homework. It's quieter than their dormitories. As you can see, we have quite a few used books that have been sent to us over the years." Dolores observed the shelves of books lining the four walls of the library.

Soon they were in the arcade connecting the dining room to the residence of the girls, usually referred to as the Girls Building. Dolores was shown the office near the front door and the visitor's suite nearby, where overnight guests were housed. The Matthews then took her downstairs to the basement into the two large rooms that housed the laundry area. Observing a single family sized wringer-type electric washing machine standing by itself, Dolores asked, "The clothes for one hundred people are washed in this one machine?"

"The bulk of our laundry is done at the Sanatorium, but each of the staff is assigned a different day in this room to do personal laundry and the better clothes that the children wear to church and sometimes school. The San is a little hard on some of the clothing, but the jeans and knitted shirts and tops usually come through okay," informed Ruth.

"My! That's a lot of clothes lines," observed Dolores, as she stared at the rows of lines strung from one end of the large basement rooms to the other.

"There are more lines outside, but they are seldom used because of our weather conditions here," said Ruth.

"With all the rain in summer, the icy ground in the fall, and deep snow in the winter, most of the staff prefer to hang the clothes inside," added Elwin.

After visiting the second floor and seeing young girls in varying stages of readying for bed and meeting their house parents, Dolores was then introduced to her living quarters on the first floor. It was a bedroom adjoining the C Dorm. "The little girls in this dorm are four through seven years of age. Their regular housemother is on vacation, and I'm afraid some of them are sick with the measles. We've had one of the older girls staying with them for the past two weeks, and now *she* has the measles. I hope that doesn't happen to you. Have you had the measles?" asked Ruth.

"You know," thought Dolores aloud, "I'm not sure."

"I believe we'll have to take a chance on that," said Mr. Matthews.

"Your little charges are bedded down now, Dolores, but I'll be over early in the morning to introduce you to them before breakfast. Get a good night's sleep. Elwin will bring your bags in."

And with that, Dolores was left standing alone in the room wondering if her degree in psychology had sufficiently prepared her to suddenly become the mother to all of these little girls. She could hardly call babysitting her little brother an adequate practicum for what lay ahead. She wasn't sure when jubilation would come into play here. It was as though she had just heard the spider say to the fly, "Come into my parlor. I'm serving leftover liver and onions with canned peas . . . and oh, by the way, you have a dorm of sick children to take care of." Then Dolores spied the bed and pronounced aloud, "Mmmm, how good it feels to have a bed to stretch my travel weary body onto again." Before long Mr. Matthews delivered her bags, and she was soon in her night-wear and asleep.

Dolores was awakened early in the morning by a faint knock on the door and sounds of sobbing from a child. She glanced at the alarm clock beside her bed and saw that it was 6:00 a.m. Ruth Matthews had warned her that a loud bell would resound throughout the buildings to awaken everybody in the Home. It was still too early; yet someone was awake. She quickly got out of bed and opened the door that led into the C Girls' dormitory. There stood a little girl about five or six years old in tears staring at the floor.

"Lizzie, my hair didn't turn out."

"Well, come in and let's see what we can do about it," said Dolores gently to the small child.

The little girl looked up in surprise. "Where's Lizzie?"

"I believe she is sick with the measles. I'm here to help you now. I'm Miss Morey. I'm going to be taking care of you for a while."

The little girl began to cry again and said through her tears, "Okay. Can you fix it?"

"Fix what, dear?"

"My hair. The curlers came out," she said with big tears flowing down her cheeks.

Dolores looked down at this little Eskimo girl with coarse, straight, black hair half wrapped around curlers but some strands stubbornly resisting to stay wrapped and sticking out in straight lines in all directions around her head. What am I supposed to do about this, she thought? The little girl stretched out her hands and showed Dolores two hands full of curlers, that had obviously fallen out of her hair during the night. "Well, we'll just put these curlers back in your hair," responded Dolores, hoping to reassure the child and bring the tears to a halt.

Her words were of no comfort. The child began to cry harder. "But I won't look good for Sunday School!"

"Yes, you will. Come into my room. I may have something that will make your hair curl fast." The little girl stopped sobbing and followed this new caretaker into the room. Dolores hoped she had packed the hair gel that might coax the coarse hair to stay wrapped around a curler. She poked around into her cosmetic bag, until she found the item that might solve this very first problem she was facing as a housemother. "Ahhh, here it is. We'll just re-wrap your hair around the curlers after I have put a little of this gel on the ends. Then I'll use the hairdryer on your curls to dry the gel quickly. You'll see. You'll have curls, and you'll look very nice for church."

A smile came over the child's face. "I will?"

"You bet'cha will. Come sit on this chair and we'll go right to work."

While Dolores was accomplishing this task, another knock was heard at a door. This time it was the door that opened out into the hallway. No sobs were heard but an adult voice saying, "Dolores, are you up?"

Dolores recognized the voice of Ruth Matthews, and answered, "Yes. Come on in."

Ruth opened the door and seeing the scene taking place in Dolores' room said, "Well, I see you've met one of your charges already. The wake-up bell will ring any minute, and I thought I would come over a little early to be here to introduce you to your dorm."

"Thanks, I appreciate that. We had an emergency here with curlers falling out, but it looks like the curling gel and my hair dryer are going to remedy the situation."

Ruth walked into the room and approached the little girl. "Well, aren't you lucky that your new housemother brought all this stuff to fix your hair?" The child gave a contented smile and shook her head yes.

"Oops! Don't move," warned Dolores and to Ruth she said, "Coarse hair doesn't want to wrap. How did her housemother do it?"

"Pat does wonders with these girls. Curls all their hair and somehow finds the time to iron all their starched dresses with ruffles and full skirts to wear to Sunday School and in the afternoon, often takes them on long walks."

"Miz Gibson bakes special treats for us too," added the child.

"You like that don't you, Suzy?" responded Ruth. Much to Dolores' dismay, Suzy nodded her head in the affirmative causing the coarse hair strand to jump out of Dolores' captive hands.

"She reads to us too."

Suddenly there came a deafening and long, loud sound of a bell ringing throughout the Home. Running feet on two floors of the building followed immediately. Dolores chuckled, "No sleepyheads in this building, I guess. They all sound eager to start the day." Dolores suddenly realized that she was still in her gown and thought herself improperly dressed to meet her dorm of girls and expressed this thought to Ruth.

"Tell you what. You finish with Suzy, and I'll go supervise the other C Girls until you're through here and can get dressed. I'm sure you'll feel more comfortable meeting them in your street clothes."

"Would you do that? Thank you so much."

When the last curl was completed and the heat from the hair dryer did its magic on the gelled ends, Dolores dismissed the little girl, who ran back into the dorm to join the others exclaiming, "She fixed it! We got a new housemother, and she fixed my hair!" Curiously, a bevy of little girls began to move towards the door from which Suzy had come.

"Don't bother Miss Morey now. She is getting dressed," called Ruth to the gathering group. "I'll introduce her to you shortly. You go on about getting ready for breakfast." The little girls did as they were told, and Dolores felt grateful to Ruth for heading them off at the pass, while she quickly made herself presentable to meet her charges. When she walked out of her room and into the dormitory, she saw Ruth painting another little girl's body with something from a bottle.

"Oh, hello, Miss Morey. This is Clara. Clara, this is your new housemother. Her name is Miss Morey and *she* will be putting this medication on you beginning tomorrow."

"Hello, Clara. I'm happy to meet you." Dolores looked down at a little girl with big, brown, sad eyes fighting back the tears.

"H'lo," sobbed Clara shyly.

"Clara has been with us only a short while. She arrived with scabies, and Dr. Phillips says we must paint her body with this medication daily," informed Ruth. "There now, Clara, it's done. You can go get ready for breakfast. That wasn't so bad was it?" Clara made no response except to sob quietly and walk away.

"Does the medication sting?" asked Dolores.

"I'm afraid it does, but the doctor says to do it *every* day. You see scabies is caused by a microscopic mite that burrows under the skin. The female mite tunnels under the skin and lays eggs. In about twenty-one days these young mites come to the surface and make little tiny blisters. That's when scabies becomes contagious and can spread to the other girls in the dorm."

"And none of the other C Girls have it?"

"No. So far, so good."

"How did you keep it from spreading?"

"With this awful medicine. It *does* kill the mites. It's uncomfortable, but so far it works."

"Poor Clara."

Suzy came running up to Dolores holding the hand of another little Eskimo girl. "This is my friend. Her name is Leona. She's younger than me."

"Hello, Leona. I'm Miss Morey. I'm happy to meet you," said Dolores, looking at a bright eyed little girl with straight black hair, bangs, and a big friendly smile spread across her face.

"H'lo. You gonna be our housemother now?"

"She sure is," said Ruth. "At least until Miss Gibson gets back from Kansas."

"You live in Kansas?" asked Leona.

"No, I live down in Seattle, Washington. Do you know where that is?"

Still grinning from ear to ear, Leona said, "No."

Another dark haired child thrust a jar of something towards Dolores and asked, "Will you put this on me, Miss Morey?"

Dolores looked down at the mysterious jar and asked, "What is it?" Ruth stepped in with an explanation, "I bet that's the lanolin that Miss Gibson rubs into your scars, isn't it Lynn?"

Lynn nodded in agreement as Dolores accepted the jar and began to remove the lid. Turning the lid she asked, "Where are your scars, Lynn?" Lynn turned her backside to Dolores and dropped her pajama bottoms, displaying lumpy scars on the back of her legs from the tops of her thighs down.

"I'm afraid the North family's house caught on fire in Nome, and Lynn was burned badly. She needs lanolin massaged into those scars daily.

It's probably done more easily if she lies on her stomach on her bed. Is that how Miss Gibson does it, Lynn?" Lynn nodded yes.

"I'll show you her bed," said the smiling Leona, wanting to be helpful. "Lynn is my sister." Dolores followed this procession to a well made up bed. Further observance made her realize all the other beds were equally well made and standing in a row around the walls of the room. Lynn immediately climbed onto the bed and laid on her stomach. And Dolores began this first of many daily tasks required of her. As she rubbed the lanolin into the scars, she was relieved that Lynn showed no signs of discomfort in this treatment. Seeing a new adult in the dorm doing a housemother's task, others began to gather around to observe this new housemother.

"Yes, come on over," said Ruth to the nine other C Girls. "I want you to meet your new housemother . . . that is, until Miss Gibson returns." The girls quickly responded with wondering eyes that focused on Dolores and her immediate task. "You too, Lily, and Dixie. Let me have a look at those measles," added Ruth. Two little girls scrambled out of their beds and came closer pulling up their pajama tops to expose the trunks of their bodies. "Those spots are well on their way out. Neither of you look contagious. You can go to the dining room today," pronounced Ruth.

Lily and Dixie let out a sound of glee, and in spite of the curiosity of meeting a new housemother, they ran to get dressed.

"There, Lynn, I think that does it. Now you can get dressed, and I'll meet these other girls." Dolores turned and looked at the group of girls varying in ages from four to seven years.

"What's your name?" asked one arriving slightly behind the others.

"My name is Miss Morey. Why don't each of you tell me your names?" Each girl said her own name, and Dolores tried to store each in her memory, knowing full well this process would need repetition. Suddenly that loud bell rang again, and the girls scurried toward the door that led into the hallway.

"Remember, no running in the halls or the arcade," reminded Ruth. And to Dolores she said, "I'll take you to your table into the dining room and introduce you to your boys and girls. The C Girls are seated among all of the other children at meals, and a housemother is assigned to each table with five children. You will of course sit at Miss Gibson's table."

"Fine," said Dolores, and she followed Ruth into the hall, feeling the curious glances from girls of all ages, wondering who the stranger was with Mrs.Matthews. Moving through the arcade, Ruth made introductions, as they came upon other staff members.

The Jesse Lee Home dining room. Photo from Rachel Yokel's collection.

Walking into the large airy dining room with thriving green plants growing heartily in the bright sunshine at the windows, Dolores smelled warm toast, and the sight of boxes of dry cereal on each of the tables around the room assured her there would be no gastronomic surprises at this meal.

But as she observed this large family of one hundred quickly taking their places at the tables around the room, she wondered what surprises they had in store for her. Would their problems be insurmountable for her lack of experience? Then her eyes fell on Suzy across the room excitedly showing her curls to the staff person at her table. Dolores smiled. Hadn't she solved that very first problem? She was ready.

Chapter 4

DOLORES...TO STAY OR NOT TO STAY

Dolores was now in her second week as a housemother. She was pleased and somewhat surprised at how quickly and comfortably she had moved into the expected routines in this new role. Two of the little girls had spent the past few days confined to the dorm, due to the measles. This situation had kept Dolores busy creating ways to reduce boredom during their recuperation. She read to them, and they read to her. She played games with them and coaxed the recovered girls to do the same. But how was she to find time to iron all of those Sunday dresses and care for the sick as well? The little girls with measles solved that problem by asking to listen to the large collection of storytelling record albums. So, as Dolores ironed and they listened, the measles slowly faded to light pink and soon became history. Becoming a housemother hadn't been easy. Her magic with Suzy's hair hadn't worked as well on some of the other girls. Due to the limitation of time and so many lost curlers in the night, some girls went off to church the second Sunday with a temporary, deflated self image. Well, what could she do? If she had to accept defeat for something as a housemother, that wouldn't leave much of a blotch on her record.

A week later, when she thought she had nursed the last girl back to health, Leona came down with a high fever and no other symptoms except a stomach ache. When the fever reached 104 degrees, Dolores ran to the office. *Is this child going to die on my watch?* she panicked in thought.

"Which girl is it?" asked Ruth.

"It's Leona!"

"Well, just keep a close watch on her. If it continues, let us know."

"But 104 degrees is very high!" Dolores insisted.

"What we have found with Leona is that she is prone to high fevers. Never lasts long, and shortly, she is usually up and about, as though nothing has happened. Just keep a close eye on her and let us know of any change."

Dolores was not sure Ruth was taking Leona's condition seriously. She was ready to call an ambulance (if Seward had such a thing) or at the least, put her in a car and take her to the doctor. However, Ruth kept reassuring Dolores that Leona would get better in short time. That was Leona's pattern. The doctor had been summoned once before but by the time he arrived, Leona was out of bed and playing. That time it had taken them ten minutes to locate her. She had approached the doctor with a big, beautiful, healthy smile saying curiously, "Hi! You come to see me?"

And now, when Dolores arrived back in the dorm, Leona was sitting up in bed playing paper dolls. "Hi, Miss Morey. You wanna play paper dolls?" Dolores quickly placed her hand on Leona's forehead and thought she felt a reduced temperature.

"How are you feeling, Leona? Feeling better?"

"Uh huh." She then raised a paper doll with a new garment for Dolores to see. "Pretty dress, huh, Miss Morey?"

"Very pretty," Dolores quietly sighed. Two hours later Leona's fever was almost down to normal.

The responsibility Dolores dreaded most was painting Clara's body with the daily medication. No matter how she applied it, Clara sobbed throughout. Surely there was a better way to treat scabies. Finally Dolores went to the office and told the Matthews of what Clara had gone through every day since her arrival. "I feel like a torturer, as that child sobs all the way through the treatment. Surely there is some alternative to this."

"Pull Clara's file, Ruth. I think we got a directive on her treatment right before Pat went on vacation," responded Elwin Matthews.

Sure enough, right there in the file was hidden the directive to cease that horrible medication quite some time ago. "Looks like we've had a breakdown in communication, what with Pat leaving and you coming. I'm sorry about that, Dolores."

Dolores was not pleased. She turned abruptly and left the office saying, "Clara will be happy to have this torture cease." Dolores couldn't hang around for another word. She was so angry, she thought she might yell or cry. Back in her room, she sat on the edge of the bed and fought the tears. *"I don't care how busy they are, that's inexcusable!"* When calm was restored, she went looking for Clara. There she was, sitting on Leona's bed playing paper dolls.

Wearing a big smile across her face, Dolores said to the child, "Clara, I have good news for you."

"What?" asked Clara with a curious expression.

"I just checked in the office and learned that we don't need to put that medication on you anymore."

Clara quickly dropped the paper doll on the bed and ran to Dolores, throwing her arms around her middle. "Oh, thank you, Miss Morey! Thank you."

Dolores was a little startled at this display of emotion, yet she realized it was merited and was a wonderful change from the lack of joy in which Clara had seemed entrapped. "I knew that would make you happy, and I'm happy about it too." She returned Clara's hug and felt a genuine bond of appreciation growing.

That night in her room, before turning out the light and closing the book she was reading, Dolores glanced at the clock. *Uh oh, I'd better wake Jodie before she wets the bed. Not that it will do any good, but we'll keep trying.* As she tiptoed into the large dorm room, all little heads appeared sound asleep. She even heard a snore or two. She reached Jodie's bed and, leaning over, tapped her on the shoulder saying, "Jodie, Jodie, time to get up and go to the bathroom." The little girl drowsily raised her head and became aware of what she was being asked to do.

"Okay, I'm going." Jodie swung her legs over the side of her bed.

"Here are your slippers," said Dolores, as she slid them under the child's feet. It was an Alaskan summer night with light still creeping through the windows, so there was no need for a flashlight to guide Jodie's steps to the bathroom. Jodie was back shortly and probably half way into slumber before Dolores settled in for the night. In the 1950's enuresis or bed wetting in a children's Home was a frustrating situation. Although Dolores had read about it in textbooks, here she was meeting it face to face. There was no cure for this problem that, more often than not, left a child with a cloak of humiliation, for there was no way to hide the wet bedding from her dorm mates. The other girls didn't understand why Jodie couldn't just stop "acting like a baby." They had.

Dolores turned out the light and rolled over with a silent prayer, that Jodie could make it through the rest of this night with a dry bed. Sometimes she did and sometimes she didn't.

The next morning Ruth came to Dolores and said, "Dolores, that candy has arrived that you wanted. It's a lot. I hope you plan to share."

"A 'chocoholic' share?! You gotta be kidding," laughed Dolores, as she followed Ruth to collect her purchase. Ruth opened the big hall closet on the first floor near the front door of the Girls Building. Candies were stored here and given to the children, as housemothers saw fit. "Here's your box of chocolate kisses. Be frugal in giving them out. We won't be placing another order for quite some time. Contributions for Christmas candies are coming in already from churches in the Lower 48."

"Lower 48?"

"Haven't heard that yet? That's what Alaskans call the continental United States."

"I see. Tell me what I owe you. I'm moving these to *my* room. It is my own personal stash, but I may share with the girls now and then, when it seems a very, very, special treat is due."

Dolores thanked Ruth and returned to her dorm, stashing the candy away in her room before checking the C Girls' Saturday work.

The chocolate kisses became a comfort food for Dolores to soften the frustrations of settling squabbles and of listening to the constant tattling and bickering a housemother faced on a daily basis. The little girls never knew of this secret stash. It became a great source of pleasure for Dolores to enjoy this wonderful confection alone. As each piece of the chocolate melted in her mouth, Dolores felt a brief tinge of guilt for not sharing, yet the chocolate seemed to fortify her for the next round of challenges. She assured her conscience that the girls were just as happy with non-chocolate candies. After all, didn't every peacemaker deserve some special reward?

"I'm tired of this job, Miss Morey. When are we gonna change jobs again?" asked Lily, as she maneuvered the big wide push broom over the dorm floor.

"Yeah, I'm tired of mine, too," said Dixie, passing by carrying a large wastepaper basket to be emptied.

"How long have you been doing these jobs?" asked Dolores.

"A long, long, lonnnnnnnng time," said Jodie with a dust pan and whisk broom sweeping up what the sweepers had brought to the center of the room.

"I'll let you take that up with Miss Gibson when she returns. She'll be back pretty soon."

"Ahhhhhhhhh, Miss Morey. Pleassssssssssseeeee," said Lily.

"Enough. Stop the whining. That's my decision. You keep the same jobs for housecleaning until Miss Gibson returns." The girls responded with moans and groans. Saturday was cleaning day at Jesse Lee Home. Each child had a job to do. The housemother was expected to check the completed work to be sure it was done well or at least to the best of the child's abilities. Although Dolores held them to a minimum standard of cleanliness, sometimes even that wasn't met.

"Lu! Where are you? The bathroom floor wasn't mopped," called Dolores, as she checked the room.

Lu was nearby and commented, "Uh huh! I did too."

"Well, it doesn't look clean. You'll have to do it again," said Dolores firmly.

"I did it good, Miss Morey. What's wrong with it? I don't see nothin' wrong with it."

"Look in the corners. Why there's even a dust ball in that one. There's been no mop here."

"I did it. The mop just didn't reach the corner."

"Well, you must *make* the mop reach the corner. If you can't do that, take a rag or sponge and do it with your hand. Here, try this." Lu received the rag with a frown. Dolores thought it would be so much easier to do it herself than to endure all of the whining. If a child didn't particularly like the assigned job, it was done with 'a lick and a promise,' and not much of that. For some, Saturday mornings were nothing more than monotonous hard labor, regardless of the energy or skill needed to accomplish the task. Others had a better attitude and did their work as fast as they could, so they would be free to spend most of the day in play. The authorities thought that making sure each job was done well would produce a responsible child, but now and then, just ignoring a less than acceptable cleaning and doing it over oneself, relieved a houseparent of the stress of dealing with a whining child. Just had to do that sometimes.

Saturday and Wednesday nights were also bath night in the showers or in the tubs (if a dorm had a tub). After Dolores discovered that kneeling beside the tub for each of the baths hurt her back, she made a visit upstairs to the big girls' dorm.

"Hi, Peggy. I've come to ask a favor." Peggy was a U.S.-2 from Iowa and had been at the Home for a year. She was taking care of the teenage girls, as well as being in charge of all of the new clothing and toys donated to the Home. Because her charges were big enough to do a lot of things for themselves, Peggy took on responsibilities other than just the care of her dorm.

"How can we help you?" she asked.

"I don't know how Pat Gibson does it, but I'm breaking my back leaning over the tub, scrubbing backs, and shampooing hair for these little girls."

"Ouch. You want some help, huh?"

"Do you think any of your big girls would be willing to come down to the C Dorm and help me scrub, shampoo, trim and clean nails? I really do need some help."

"Well, we've been waiting for you to call upon us. Guess Pat didn't leave the message behind that the A Girls come and help her on bath nights. Let's go get some help for you. When do you want them? Tonight?"

"Right now, to be exact. We're just about ready to start baths." Dolores followed Peggy, as she went from room to room asking the girls to come together for a brief meeting. No one big dormitory room for these girls! Some had lived at Jesse Lee Home for many years and knew that when they became of age, they merited small rooms with a roommate or two. At the gathering Dolores pled her case. Several girls raised their hands and said, "I'll do it!" So three or four A Girls followed Dolores down the stairs and into the C Dorm. The little girls were delighted to see some big sisters or perhaps a big girl from the dining table, where they sat. It was special to be the center of attention from these *big* girls. The A Girls felt special to be placed in a position of authority over these little ones. Some, of course, tried to take advantage of this new authority, but each time, Miss Morey was near-by, and kept everything well in line.

Before Dolores' month was over with the C Girls, she had the opportunity to take them on an outing up the highway. They piled into the cars of some of the staff and drove up to Lawing, Alaska, a tiny spot by the railroad very near Moose Pass. The settlement was named after Nellie Lawing, a famous elderly Alaskan pioneer. She was known as "Alaska Nellie" and was quite the character. She had written a book about herself with lots of colorful stories about hunting wild game, skinning them out, and mounting them on the walls of her log cabin. Nellie was a skilled person of the woods. Her stories revealed that she was capable of accomplishing any thing in Alaska that a man could. She did much of the building of her cabin and filled the walls with her trophies from hunting. In her younger days, she had carried the mail on horseback and dog team. Now she lived on the Kenai Peninsula in a cabin by the railroad tracks surrounded by her feats of yesteryear, enjoying the companionship of two rabbits. The huge rabbit, called "Brother," joined Nellie at the dining table for meals. Nellie proudly announced that she had that rabbit house trained. Of course the rabbits delighted the little girls, and Nellie loved having guests. It was a very pleasant afternoon for all. Before they departed, Dolores asked Nellie to autograph a book.

"Why, you've bought my book! Did you enjoy it?"

"Very much so. When I learned you were living so near Seward, your book made me want to come and meet you. Thank you for giving us such a wonderful afternoon." Nellie happily obliged with an autograph. She thanked Dolores for bringing the little girls, saying that she always enjoyed kids. As they drove back to Seward, Dolores mused that living in those big buildings at Jesse Lee was like living in a huge hotel complex in comparison to Nellie's small but cozy cabin.

The next day on Dolores' day off, she enjoyed taking a leisure bath in the staff bathroom on the second floor and not having to rush into the dorm to herd the girls through their pre-breakfast routines to get them off to the dining room on time. As she dried her body off, she noticed red spots on her belly. *What is that?* She took the hand mirror and examined her body all over. Sure enough, there were red splotches on other parts of her body. I have taken the measles, she sighed. Then she began to chuckle. Well, I guess it was bound to happen. I needn't fear that I will put the girls at risk, since they have already been exposed. After all, *they exposed me! Or was it my sleeping in Lizzie's bed, who also got the measles? Even with changed sheets, can that happen? Whatever, I've got 'em.* It turned out to be a light case of the measles.

Shortly after Dolores' discovery of the measles, Mr. Matthews dropped by to see her. "How are you coming battling those measles? I'm sure sorry we had to put you into this den of exposure. But that's the risks when working with kids."

"Oh, I'm doing fine. It doesn't seem to be a bad case. The spots on my stomach are fading already. No apology necessary."

"I appreciate your willingness to continue caring for the dorm, in spite of the measles. I just needed to check and see for myself, if that was a wise decision for you to keep working."

Dolores laughed and said, "I'm sure the other housemothers think it is a *very* wise decision. Doubling up with the care of two dorms is a real challenge."

"Yes, operating without a full staff puts a strain on everybody. I'm sorry to announce that we're just about to lose another houseparent soon."

"Oh? Who is that?" she asked curiously.

"Miss Seppin in the Boys Building is going, and that will leave the B Boys without a housemother."

"Is that the pre-teenage boys?"

"Yes." He paused. "Dolores, I have been very pleased with your work. Pat Gibson will be returning soon to a group of well cared for girls. Thank you. I would like to move you over to the Boys Building to take Miss Seppin's place."

"Why, yes. I could finish out the summer over there. Would certainly be different from caring for the little girls. No long hair to put up in curlers," she laughed. "Or frilly dresses to iron."

"That's true. I should list those as some of the benefits," he chuckled. "What are your plans, when you return to Seattle?"

"I'm not sure yet. Of course I'll have to start looking for a job when I get back."

"Well, I'd like to offer you the position of full time housemother to the B Boys. Would you consider staying on with us and taking Miss Seppin's place?"

"Oh, my! I'd have to think about that."

"Of course. Well, you think about that, and we'll talk again soon."

Once Elwin Matthews left her room, Dolores stood motionless just staring into space while thinking, well, now isn't *that* a surprise? *Stay here at Jesse Lee and not go on home at the end of the summer?* That had never even occurred to her. Suddenly she was jarred out of her thoughts with the loud clanging of the lunch bell. In the dining room this new request vied for her attention, as she served the children at her table. Once that was done, her eyes looked around the dining room searching for B Boys, wondering what it would be like to care for them. She need only look across the table at Horace. He was a B Boy and a great tease to be sure, always smiling and making the little kids laugh. He was the brother to two of the girls in her C Dorm. Horace was from a large family of children, who seemed to bear a special bond of caring about each other.

After lunch there was the usual quick chit-chat with other staff, as they prepared to return to their respective dorms. Dolores decided not to share Mr. Matthews' request with any of them yet. After all, it was a lot to think about and much to be considered. She missed Seattle . . . so much so that if a passenger ship was due to dock on one of her days off, she walked into town just to be with the crowd and see faces other than those she saw every day at the Home. Just getting around in this town was different too. Seward wasn't big enough to afford a public transportation system, so without a car, one was forced to walk everywhere in all kinds of weather. Town was at least a mile from the Home. Walking back to the Girls Building from the dining room, Dolores glanced out the windows of the long covered hallway called the arcade. Another lousy weather day in Seward, she thought. *It's funny, I never thought much about the constant rain while growing up in Seattle, but here, everything seems so bleak on rainy days. Must be the gravel and glacial silt that the kids tromp in on wet days.*

"You seem lost in thought," said Peggy, entering the arcade from the Girls Building and walking towards Dolores. "A penny for your thoughts."

"Just thinking about the weather and how cold and windy it can be here, even in the summer."

"Oh, you get used to it. I did. I was told when I arrived, 'If you don't like the weather, just wait a minute, it'll change.' And it does."

"So there *is* hope. The sun *will* shine again?" responded Dolores.

"I guarantee it, and when it does, with all of the foot traffic coming in and out of the Home, you'll have an opportunity to sweep up dust, dirt, and grit several times a day."

"So I'm beginning to notice," Dolores sighed and continued on her way. *"Hmmm, the weather is definitely a negative and come to think of it, my parents' big 25th anniversary is coming up in January. I don't want to miss that. What else would I miss? Why of course, my first presidential election! Alaska does not have statehood, and as a resident of a territory, I could not vote.* It seemed these thoughts were about to make up Dolores' mind.

As Dolores arrived near the office door, suddenly Ruth Matthews popped her head out and announced the mail had arrived. "By the way, Dolores, Elwin told me he had asked you to take Miss Seppin's place. I do hope that you will seriously consider it. You'd make a great housemother for those boys. They are ready for more structure in their existence, and I know you would handle that well."

"Thank you, I'm giving it thought." Dolores quickly moved on, not wanting to discuss the matter further at the moment. She carried a handful of mail back to her room. Seeing her home address on one envelope, she quickly opened that one. It was her mother saying:

"What a challenge you're having this summer with those little girls. I wonder what you'll be asked to do next. Whatever it is, I know you'll do a good job."

Your Dad and I miss you, but know you will head south to Seattle in the fall. Just this morning at breakfast, your brother was talking to your Dad and me about the big anniversary coming up in January. The two of them think we should invite all of the relatives from Quilcene and your Aunt Marguerite in Oregon. I don't know. This party is getting awful big. Don't you think? I told them we'd best wait until you get home to make any final plans."

"Hmmm, looks like I'm needed back home," came her nagging thoughts.

Suddenly a little girl appeared at her door. "Miss Morey, there's two mens at the door asking for you."

"Mens? Who are they?"

"I dunno."

"Did they give their names?"

"Huh uh. Just asked if you were somewhere near-by. I said I'd go get you." Curiously Dolores set the rest of her mail aside and followed the child to the dormitory door that led out into the hall. "Here she is. I toldja I'd get her." There stood Mr. Milroy out of his conductor's uniform with a handsome young man beside him.

"Hello, Dolores. We meet again. How are you?"

"Why, I'm doing fine, Mr. Milroy. How are you?"

"Couldn't be better. I'd like for you to meet my young friend here, Kyle Fields. Kyle, this is Dolores Morey."

The blonde young man smiled, "How do you do? Mr. Milroy has been talking about you for some time and just insisted that I come out here to meet you."

"Well, how nice of you to come. If you'll give me a minute, I'll get someone to watch my girls, and we'll go into the visitor's lounge and visit."

"Looks like we've inconvenienced you, and I apologize," offered Kyle. "I told you we should call first, Hugh."

"She has no phone."

"Yes, the absence of a phone in our rooms is an inconvenience for the staff with friends or acquaintances in Seward. Up to now, I really hadn't noticed that inconvenience, since Hugh Milroy is possibly the only person, outside of the Home, that I know in Seward. Well, all of Alaska to be exact."

"Well, we've just remedied that. Now you know two," responded Milroy.

"Thank you, I just wish I had more time to give to this visit. Perhaps, you two could come back on my day off."

"Well, that's what we're here for to learn such important details," said Milroy. And thus began Dolores' relationship with one of Seward's most eligible bachelors.

Chapter 5

DOLORES BECOMES THE
B BOYS' HOUSEMOTHER

Dolores sat in the office looking across the desk at Elwin Matthews. "I'm eager to hear your decision, Dolores. What is it?"

Elwin Matthews, Superintendent of Jesse Lee Home, 1952. Photo from Rachel Yokel's collection.

"Well, in thinking it over, it's true that I have no other job offer at this time, and since you have generously offered to let me return home briefly in January to attend my parents' anniversary, I will accept the longer term assignment as housemother to the B Boys."

"That's wonderful. Thank you, Dolores, I'm very pleased. I take it the boys haven't been too hard on you, since you went over there after Pat returned from vacation."

"Well, the first thing they asked me was, "Where is your car?" They miss Miss Seppin's van and I'm afraid . . . all those opportunities to go on outings that require a vehicle."

"Yes, they got spoiled in that respect, but they'll adjust. How are their sanitation habits and dorm cleaning skills?"

"A bit relaxed about both," Dolores chuckled. "Tell you the truth, some of those little girls in the C Dorm can out work a lot of those B Boys."

"I was afraid of that, but I know you'll bring about a change there."

"I'll try. I'm already expecting more from them on personal cleanliness. Some are not too happy that the new housemother keeps a close check on their appearance. 'Miss Seppin never made us wash our necks over,' some have complained. Then too, they aren't happy that I have no interest in fishing. 'Miss Sepppin took us fishing,' they've been lamenting. She's a hard act to follow."

"There are plenty of places to fish near-by. They don't need a van to transport them."

B Boys with fish. Photo from Rachel Yokel's collection.

"So I discovered. On my first day over there with those boys, some asked to go to the beach, without me of course. Since I never let the C Girls leave the grounds without me, I was very hesitant, but the boys insisted that Miss Seppin always let them go alone. I realize that they really are older than the C Girls. After all, these boys are upper elementary students, so I let them go, but I had anxiety about it. Before too long they were back exclaiming, 'Miss Morey, we brought you a gift!' They stood there grinning from ear to ear holding a very long pole. At the far end was dangling a long-dead king crab. The reason for the length of the pole became obvious; even they couldn't stand the smell."

Mr. Matthews broke out into laughter, "Dolores, I'm afraid you'll be in for a lot of practical jokes from these boys. If it gets too bad, let me know."

"I'll keep that in mind," she said, as she stood up to leave.

Mr. Matthews stood too. "So glad you're on board with us," he smiled. "Let me know if you need anything."

"Thank you. You may be hearing from me sooner than you think." With that, Dolores left the office chuckling and returned to the Boys Building. Walking up the stairs to the second floor, she felt a breeze flowing through the building from open windows here and there. Suddenly her nose picked up a scent suggestive of uncleanliness. *Now what is that, and where is it coming from?* She walked past her room at the top of the stairs and stuck her head in the boys' bathroom across the hall. No, no unpleasant smells in there, so she went all the way to the end of the hall and opened the door to the gym on the right. A few boys were playing one on one throwing the basketball around. No, that smell definitely was not sweaty gym clothes. What was it? She crossed the hall and went into the large room of the B Boys' dorm. There it was! The windows were open, and it was certainly something in *that* room. "What *is* that horrible smell in here?" she asked of the few boys milling around the big room.

"What smell?" asked one of the boys.

"I don't smell nothin'," commented another. The others just looked at each other and shrugged their shoulders.

"I want the source of that mysterious smell found in one hour, or after supper, every single one of these lockers will be cleaned out and scrubbed." She walked out returning to her room, hoping the boys would uncover whatever was causing the foul odor. It seemed 'clean' was a dirty word to boys of this age, and some would go to any length to protect themselves from it. *What is wrong with their noses? That smell would gag a maggot.*

Very soon the dinner bell rang, and the thunder of rapidly moving feet of boys in four dorms moving through the halls, descending the stairs, and heading into the arcade towards the dining room filled her ears. I really do believe this building is noisier than the Girls Building, she thought, as she washed her hands vigorously, as though that would remove some of the obnoxious smell. Dolores decided that after dinner she would check the room again and if the smell remained, she would order the boys to clean the lockers. Why wait any longer? During dinner word spread fast that Miss Morey was going to make the boys clean lockers; Miss Seppin had never asked them to do *that*. Once the meal was over, B Boys, who had other plans for their evening, surrounded Miss Morey and asked, "Is it true? Do we have to scrub down our lockers?"

"You certainly do, if you don't find the source of that awful smell?"

"Come on! Let's go look for it. I may know what it is!" one of the boys said to the others and darted off to start the big search. When Dolores reached the dorm, most of the boys were in a searching mode looking under beds and behind chests of drawers and other furniture.

"Have your lockers ever been emptied and scrubbed with soap and water?" she asked of the entire room. The boys stopped searching momentarily, and some shook their heads back and forth to indicate no. "Then this is as good a time as any. Clean your lockers."

"Wait, Miss Morey. I bet this is it!" The boy raised a coffee can that had been tucked away in the corner at the back of the room.

"Let me see," she ordered the child. He brought the tin to her and thrust it towards her nose. "Phew! That's a rotting fish! How long has that been there?" Of course it was a mystery. Several were accused, but none owned up to storing their fresh catch from the week before in the coffee tin. That was enough. Dolores decided that once the dead fish was disposed of, there would be a summit conference to set down rules on fishing. With the rotten fish removed from the dorm, the breeze flowing through the windows carried the smell of elderberry bushes in bloom. Ahhh, now that is more like it, thought Dolores. Before bed time, she invited all of the boys into her large spacious room at the opposite end of the hall. Her windows brought forth the awesome view of mountains surrounding Resurrection Bay and Seward in the distance. She had to admit that the view helped her decide to honor Mr. Matthews' request to stay. It being bedtime, the boys came in their pajamas, and the conference on fishing began. There was much discussion on the size of the fish that could be kept. That became rule number one. Dolores came up with the next most important rule; fish must be kept in a *proper* storage place before eating. In fact, she pretty much dominated the rest of the discussion with rules three and four; fish must be *dead* and cleaned before taken to the kitchen for storage in the refrigerator, and no more tiny live fish swimming frantically in the bathroom sinks.

After lunch on Thursdays, the kids returned to school, as the housemothers all came together in what was called the laundry sorting room in the Girls Building. Large tables were there for sorting clothes, but the staff usually sat on benches around the wall with huge cotton bags of

Jesse Lee Home staff sorting clothes. From left to right Ruth Matthews, wife of the superintendent, Gladys Bollinger, B Girls' housemother, Rachel Yokel, C Boys' housemother, and Pat Gibson, C Girls' housemother. Photo from Rachel Yokel's collection.

children's clean clothing in front of them. Each garment had a dorm's colored tag sewn into the waist of trousers and at the neck line of other clothing. The sewing of tags had been done by the kids or the house-mothers for the younger children. Although the tuberculosis sanatorium laundry staff received the dirty laundry segregated by these colored tags, they never bothered to keep the items separated when washing them. So the cleaned clothes were packed for return in a mish-mash of colored tags. It was up to the housemothers to pull each garment from the bags and separate the items into piles, according to the proper dorm color.

The bed linens came ironed and folded, and Peggy, along with Ruth (when she could break away from the office), took on the job of sepa-rating the linens on the large tables per the seven dorm areas. This weekly procedure became a few hours of socializing for the staff without their charges around. Actually this chore became fun, as clothing was pulled from the bags and garments began to fly through the air and hopefully, landing on the correct designated piles. Once separated by colored tags, the clothes were re-stuffed into the individual giant laundry bags and left in the middle of the floor of the laundry sorting room. After school the big A Boys carried the heavy bags to the proper dorms.

On this particular Thursday, Gladys, the B Girls' housemother, pulled out a pair of jeans and held them up in the air for all to see. No tag! Who claims them?"

"Oh, those belong to Horace! I know! I'll take them!" called Dolores from across the room.

Pat laughed, "How can you be so sure, Dolores, without a name or tag in them?"

"Oh, jeans have a tendency to take on the identity of the wearer, contours and all. Look at them. That's Horace!"

"Hmmm. Maybe so," remarked Gladys. "Don't think I can identify the B Girls' jeans that way. That's uncanny how you can do that, Dolores."

"Oh, just one of my many talents. What can I say?" and the room fell into laughter.

Following the sorting, some of the staff gathered into the adjoining room for tea. This room was designated the staff kitchen and was off limits to the kids. Lively conversation continued, and again, Ruth

Matthews would take a break from the office and join them. The staff shared the humorous antics of their charges, as well as their problem situations. In this way, they caught up on the latest happenings in each of the dorms and what was occurring on the days off of the staff. Phyllis, the relief housemother in the Girls Building, popped the question every one was eager to ask, "How's the new boy friend coming, Dolores? What's he like?"

"Yes," said Peggy, "surely you realize that all of us 'spinsters' must live vicariously through you. Tell us about it."

"We are assuming that you had quite a date with him on your last day off," Rachel, the C Boys' housemother, commented in a teasing manner.

"Obviously, not much gets past the awesome perception of this group. Let me tell you about it. It was *horrible*."

"No! What? Really?" came the response to that unexpected remark.

"This is an outdoorsman quite eager to show me the great Alaskan outdoors. So he suggested, 'Let's take a walk up Mt. Marathon.' "

"A walk?" commented Ruth. "Sounds more like a *hike* to me. Elwin and I took our boys up that trail. I hardly made it to the tree line. It's steep."

Dolores laughed, "Tell me about it! But as it turned out, the steepness was the least of our troubles, although that was trouble enough. About half way up the mountain, I said, 'Kyle, let's rest. I've got to catch my breath.' 'Fine,' he said and we sat down on the side of the trail. At this point he took a candy bar out of his pocket and offered it to me. 'Here, this will give you some energy. You like chocolate?' I all but grabbed it out of his hand."

"Thus far, this sounds like a great Sunday afternoon . . . a stroll up the mountain and a chocolate bar besides. Nothing horrible about this story," remarked Rachel.

"Just you wait. No sooner did I have the wrapping off, when out of nowhere, came this young black bear right in front of us! 'Don't move!' said Kyle. How could I move? We both froze!"

"Did he get your candy bar?" asked Phyliss.

"No!" said Peggy. "I hope not. You are not supposed to give the bears food. That tells them people are an easy touch for food!"

"So, what did you do?" asked Gladys.

"The bear seemed to freeze also. Guess it was as startled as we were. 'Put the candy away,' Kyle said quickly but quietly, and to the bear, he said calmly, 'Go away, bear. Go find your mama. Go away.' He kept saying that over and over again. The bear grunted and looked puzzled, while I shivered in my boots. Never had I been so close to a bear out of captivity."

"Then what?" asked Ruth.

"Kyle stood up slowly keeping his eyes focused on the bear. Suddenly I felt abandoned down on the ground at eye level with this small bear, so I began to stand, but I felt a gentle push from Kyle, as he said, 'Stay down. We don't want the bear to think we're aggressive. Its mother could be nearby.' The thought of another and larger bear ready to pounce to protect this one had my nerves unraveling. This was not my kind of a pleasant Sunday afternoon."

"So are you going to tell us that Kyle shot the bear?" asked Pat.

"No, he wasn't carrying a gun, to my knowledge. The bear didn't appear comfortable with Kyle standing, so the bear backed up a few steps and then moved off the trail a few feet. Kyle then helped me to my feet and said, 'Let's slowly move on up the trail.' I really wanted to move *down* the trail with haste and call it a day, but it appeared the bear was headed in that direction. We made it up to the tree line and there, finally enjoyed the chocolate bars. Kyle found another route down, but I was a wreck, and never relaxed for a moment until we got back to his car."

"Well, look at it this way, Dolores, your gentleman caller gave you the exciting experience of seeing an Alaskan bear," chuckled Rachel.

"You know something, Rachel, I think I could have managed without that exciting moment and not feel the least slighted," she said laughingly.

"You're lucky the mother bear was not around, or this story could have had a different ending," said Peggy.

"That's what Kyle said once we were back in the car with the doors closed."

"So that was your horrible date," commented Ruth smiling. "What else does this outdoorsman have planned for your Alaskan adventures?"

"Nothing outdoors, let me tell you! He wants to make it up to me and take me to a steak dinner . . . *indoors*."

"Gabe's?" asked Phyliss. "I've been there. You'll like that . . . unless he offers you bear steak," she laughed.

"I saw cows in the meadows on the day we drove up to Jesse Lee from the train station, so with cows in this town, I'm counting on Gabe serving beef steak."

"I'm sure that's what you'll get, but if Gabe's been hunting, he likes to offer his customers a bite of what he's shot."

"What's the latest news from the office, Ruth?" asked Gladys. "Anything interesting?"

"Anything as exciting as Dolores' bear story?" chuckled Pat.

"Well, Rachel might think so. The Woman's Division has informed us that we are getting another U.S.-2 the last of the summer. That should free Rachel up from being a full-time housemother in the Boys Building and let her get on with the group work she was hired to do. Elwin gave Peggy the name and address and asked that she write to a fellow U.S. - 2. Have you heard back from her, Peggy?"

"Yes, as a matter of fact, just yesterday. She's from Tennessee, and her name is Betty Jane Epps. She asked all of the typical questions. Wants to know about the weather and if we speak English to the kids. I sent her a list of the names of the D Boys. Guess she'll be taking care of the youngest boys, right?" she asked of Ruth.

"That's the plan right now," responded Ruth.

"I'm delighted she's coming. It seems eons since we've had a full staff," said Rachel. The others nodded in agreement. "I hope we can scour up enough furniture to put in her room. We've been short handed for so long, we've taken furniture from unused staff rooms and given it to active staff. Anybody have any pieces of furniture you can bear to do without?" No immediate offers came forth.

"Maybe the maintenance men can find some scraps of furniture. We'll have to tell them to be on the lookout," commented Ruth.

"Want me to do that?" asked Rachel. "We're through here now. I can do that. It will probably be my task to get her room ready anyway."

"Thanks, Rachel. You've read my mind. I've got some more work to do in the office this afternoon and must get on with it."

"Sure." Rachel and Ruth stood up to leave, and the others began to gather teacups and place them in the sink.

Before Dolores could leave the room, Mr. Matthews appeared at the door and asked, "Miss Morey, could you spare me a few B Boys on Saturday to help in harvesting the garden? Those root crops are ready to come out of the ground, and some of the berries need to be picked."

"I think that can be arranged. By the way, the boys have told me many times that they much prefer planting, weeding, hoeing, and harvesting to the Saturday housecleaning of sweeping, dusting, and the like. How many of them do you want?"

"You can send me the four oldest boys or four good workers. I'll have the A Boys there as well. Want them ready to go right after breakfast."

"I'll see that you have them." As Dolores walked back to her domain, she was glad Mr. Matthews had asked for her boys. There wasn't an abundance of good male role models. At this time of the season, the garden work was totally a man's world. When really needed, she understood the A Girls were called in to help, but this Saturday it would just be the guys.

The boys who were not chosen to go to work in the garden with Mr. Matthews were miffed. Dolores had to endure lots of grumbling that day, even though she worked side by side with the boys, as they did the extra work of the chosen four.

Dolores Morey, B Boys' Housemother, helping one of her boys clean a shower.

"Miss Morey, can we play cowboys and Indians after lunch?" asked Maurice. Dolores looked at this Aleut child wondering what he knew of the plains culture in the Lower 48.

"*May* we," she corrected.

Maurice grinned and repeated, "*May* we?"

"If you boys get your work done before the lunch bell rings, you may play anything you like this afternoon." A loud exclamation of glee came forth from all of the boys within hearing distance of her voice. Horace exited quickly and could be heard telling the other B Boys the good news. Dolores was a little puzzled that granting that request brought such joy. *Do they know . . . something that I don't?* she pondered. Her permission turned out to be quite the motivator, as the boys put extra energy into their chores, and each one had asked her to check their completed jobs before the lunch bell clanged.

When Dolores returned from lunch, some of the boys were waiting at the closed door to her room. Curiously, she asked, "Why are you boys gathered here at my door?"

"We want the paints," responded Maurice.

"Paints? What paints?" asked Dolores.

"The ones in your closet. Miss Sepppin said she would leave'em behind," offered Horace. Oh, yes. Dolores remembered seeing a box of several sets of water color paints in her closet and had wondered about them.

"You want to paint pictures? Changed your minds? I thought you wanted to play cowboys and Indians."

"We do!" they seemed to all shout at once.

"Then what are the paints for?" At that moment Clyde appeared with all of his clothes removed except for a muffler strategically placed around his body like a loin cloth. "Clyde! What have you done? Why are you dressed . . . or should I say undressed like that!"

"It's my turn to be an Indian. Where are the paints?"

"She hasn't given'em to us yet," responded his brother Horace.

"And just what do you plan to do with the paints?"

"Paint our bodies!" came the answers in unison.

"It's war paint," said Clyde. "Half of us are cowboys, and half of us are Indians. We take turns each time we get to play."

Hmmm, thought Dolores in surprise. Maybe these boys know more about the culture of the early western states than I realized. She looked at their eager faces and wondered what the afternoon had in store for her. "Wait here. I'll go look for them."

"Miss Seppin kept 'em on the bottom shelf!" called Horace, still standing outside the door.

"How do you know?" questioned his older brother.

"Cause one time she sent me in there to get 'em." The others looked at him enviably. Shortly Dolores was back carrying a large box marked Water Colors and Brushes. "This must be it," she said as she handed the box to Clyde's outstretched arms.

"Thanks, Miss Morey!" said Clyde with all of the others joining in. The group quickly dispersed, some to the bathroom to start the painting and others to the dorm to get the 'breechcloths.' Within an hour the hall was filled with war painted Indians and cowboys carrying sticks for guns, making the sound of those noisy weapons that in turn, produced war cries from the 'Indians.' Dolores noted that some of the artwork on the 'Indians' was quite good, and obviously, some had enjoyed being painted from head to toe. Once the last 'Indian' was painted, the games had begun. Feet running in all directions and blood curdling yells turned a quiet Saturday afternoon into a battle on the prairie with the 'Indians' on the warpath.

I consented to this? Dolores asked herself. The next time I'm asked if they can play cowboys and Indians in this rather extreme way, I won't be so quick to say yes. She put up with this wild play for about an hour and a half and yet, neither of the two housemothers for the two dorms on the first floor or the one above on the third floor ever made an appearance to complain about the noise. For the last thirty minutes she shooed them off to a new war zone in the gym and closed the door. The war cries and running feet were somewhat muffled but still could be heard. It was like turning the volume down on a western movie filled with action. Finally, after two hours, she called a halt to the noisy play and sent all of the 'Indians' to the showers to remove the war paint. From that day on, the box of paints and brushes were placed in the big dorm room with a stack of plain paper with the suggestion from Dolores, that they use the paints in a quieter and more creative way. However, the boys weren't beyond taking advantage of Miss Morey's day off and talking the relief house-mother into letting them return to the wild west. Also, with the paints readily at their disposal, when word got around that Miss Morey had submerged herself into a well deserved hot bath, they knew she would not interrupt that long pleasure to demand a peace treaty be signed by the opposing forces, and thus restore calm on the second floor. Once submerged, her tolerance surfaced. The war cries began, and she knew Custer was going to get it one more time but certainly without interference from this housemother.

* * *

Mr. Matthews announced to his staff that the territorial health department recommended a first-aid class be offered. Realizing the importance of such training, the staff diligently studied the manual and moved through the hands-on training that could save a life. It was a lot to learn, and all hoped it would never be necessary to actually use. Well, that became a hollow wish in a children's Home. The very next week after the training was completed, Dolores had an occasion to call upon the first-aid facts she had stored in her head.

On rainy days the gym was very popular, as all of the children needed a chance to rid themselves of excess energy. Roller skates gave that opportunity. Some of the boys weren't content to simply skate but combined it with playing basketball. Basketball on roller skates? Don't think I have ever heard of anybody doing that in Seattle, thought Dolores. When she popped her head into the gym, she noticed the game was played hard and fast and again, very noisily. She was about to close the door and leave the boys to another extreme way of playing, when a hard, loud sound caught her attention. It appeared that Horace was skating so fast, that he hit the wall behind the basket and knocked the wind out of himself. When she got to him, he was lying on the floor in pain, and his dark black hair was standing straight up on his head from the impact. Rachel was summoned, and the two of them thought the worst. Finally they decided to chance moving him in order to get to the doctor in town. With much caution, he was carried down the stairs by the A Boys and placed in the back seat of Mr. Matthews' car. As Mr. Matthews drove the one mile to the hospital, Horace lay quietly without a sound with Rachel watching from the front passenger seat. Sometime later, Mr. Matthews deposited him on the steps of the Boys Building all bandaged up around his rib cage. Rachel escorted Horace to Dolores, saying the doctor advised that Horace take it easy for the next two weeks. Horace displayed a lot of notable discomfort, as she tried to help him get into his pajamas. Then she brought him a glass of water and two aspirins. Observing him in such pain, she figured the broken rib would keep him subdued for awhile. She brought him his supper from the dining room and helped him sit up to eat, stacking pillows behind him to bring as much comfort as possible under the circumstances.

After the chaos of the wild Indians and cowboys taking over the hallway, Dolores had long since laid down the law of no running in the halls. The morning following the accident in the gym, she was awakened by the sound of running feet, that seemed to be coming from the dorm to the B Boys' bathroom and back again. The early morning light had awakened some of the boys before the wake-up bell rang, and they were ready to start their day, whether the Home was or not. The running continued. Dolores got out of bed, put on her robe and stepped outside her door. No sooner had she done that, then here came Clyde running at break neck speed with, of all things, Horace in hot pursuit behind him. "Horace! What are you doing? The doctor told you to take it easy. Is this what you call taking it easy?" Both boys stopped abruptly. "Besides disobeying the doctor's orders, you are waking people out of a sound sleep before it is time to get up."

"Sorry," both boys said meekly.

"You *know* running in the halls is breaking the rules. Clyde, I'm surprised at you. Is this how you help your brother heal from a broken rib?"

"He said it didn't hurt this morning," offered Clyde.

"I think this bandage is too loose," said Horace, as he held up one end of a dangling bandage.

"Oh, dear. Let me see. Come on into my room, and I'll try to put it back the way it was. All that running no doubt loosened it." Horace stood guiltily before his housemother pulling his pajama top up above his rib cage. The bandages were hanging loosely around his chest. "Take off your pajama top, and I'll try to fix it." Dolores removed the entire length of bandaging and rewrapped his rib cage as snuggly as she dared. "How is the pain this morning?"

"Not much."

She took a safety pin from her desk drawer and pinned the final loose end in place. "There. That should keep it from hanging loose again." She then lectured him on the importance of caring for his wounded body and gave him some explanation of the meaning of 'taking it easy.' If he took her advice, it wasn't noticeable, as he returned to active play after breakfast, and from that point on, one would never have known that he had an injury.

Her newly trained Red Cross First-Aid skills were put into use another time, when Clyde came in from playing on the mountain side with his pants torn and dirty. "What has happened to you?" she inquired.

"I fell and tore my pants."

He wasn't limping, so she assumed he was okay. "Well, take them off and put them in the laundry. I'll see if I can mend your pants when they are clean." Clyde quickly changed into clean pants and went on his way. Later in the day, she noticed blood stains in the area of his upper thigh on one leg in those clean jeans. "Clyde, do you realize your leg is bleeding? Look at your jeans."

Clyde looked down at the blood stains. "Guess I must have cut myself when I fell."

"Did you wash that wound when you changed pants?"

"No."

"Then take those pants off. I want to see that wound."

"Oh, it's okay, Miss Morey. It's not bleeding much."

"It's bleeding enough to soil your pants. Come into my room and let me look at that wound."

"It's okay, Miss Morey. It's not bad."

"Clyde, I insist. I need to examine that wound." Clyde reluctantly followed his housemother into her room and slowly removed his pants. Dolores caught her breath when she saw a bleeding puncture wound about one half inch across. She quickly grabbed her First-Aid Kit and cleaned the wound as best she could. "Clyde, we have no idea how deep this wound is. I think a doctor needs to take a look at this." And he was soon whisked off to the doctor in town, who filled the wound with penicillin and then took a couple of stitches. Mr. Matthews escorted Clyde to Dolores and told Clyde to tell his housemother what the nurse had said.

"Uh, she said I should wash a cut as soon as I get one."

"And tell her why," prompted Mr. Matthews.

"Cause it could get infected."

"I do hope that you have learned something from this experience, Clyde, and there will be no more ignoring bloody pants. Thank you, Mr. Matthews, for taking him to the doctor." The boy shook his head indicating that he had been duly warned and started off to look for his peers.

"So, Dolores, otherwise, how are things coming over here in the Boys Building for you?"

"I'm glad you asked. Come, I want to show you something." She led him down the hall to the B Boys' dorm. "Look at all of these windows."

"Sure allows a lot of light in the room, doesn't it?"

"Too much. There isn't one shade on any of these tall windows. The boys go to bed with the sun still shining through them, and this room is flooded with light through most of the Alaskan summer nights. It's hard for them to ignore all of this light and go off to sleep."

"It's creating a problem?"

"I'll say! I used to be able to sleep six or seven hours each night in the Girls Building but not over here. By 1:30 or 2:00 in the morning, jillions of seagulls are on the roof screeching and seem to be saying, 'Time to get up! Time to get up!' With the morning sun shining in their eyes, and the beckoning call of the seagulls, one half of these boys are up and moving around. At first they were running with abandonment up and down the halls laughing and playing. That woke the other half, as well as me. I put a stop to that, and now I tell them to get a book and read if they can't sleep. These boys are not getting as much sleep as they need."

"I'm sure there were shades on these windows at one time, but where they are now, I have no idea," remarked Mr. Matthews.

"May I request that black-out shades be purchased for this dorm?"

"That would involve a large amount of money for this many windows. Money I'm afraid we don't have."

"I see them as an absolute necessity. Short of hanging blankets over the windows, a monumental task, what can we do?"

"I sympathize with the situation, and it's a budgetary problem I'll have to take on. I can't promise any immediate solution, but I will take it under consideration."

"If we can't afford black-out shades, we'll settle for any kind of shades to reduce the light in the room."

"I understand but right now there is no money available for either. I'll inform the New York Mission office of this need, but all of this takes time . . . just like the painting of the buildings. But it looks like that is actually going to happen within the next year. You wouldn't believe how long that request has been in."

"Well, you told me to let you know if I needed any help, and there it is."

"I'll do my best. We can at least put in the request."

"Thank you. I appreciate that."

"Keep an eye on Clyde and let me know if there are any further concerns. I think he got the message loud and clear from the doctor's office on when to take care of a wound."

"Thanks. Let's hope so." And they went their separate ways.

Dolores discovered that if she read to the boys at bed time, it had a calming effect, and that helped, in spite of the light pouring into the room. She bargained with them that she would read any book they chose in exchange for a modicum of quiet following the reading. They grew to love her reading aloud at the end of their day, and each seemed to be adjusting to the new demands of a different housemother. Institutional living simply required flexibility. Dolores mused, how many times would that quality be necessary in their lifetime at Jesse Lee Home?

Chapter 6

BETTY JANE ARRIVES

I was seated in the front of the big plane that was taking me to Anchorage. In fact, I was very near to the door of the pilot's cabin. There was only one stewardess manning the single aisle, and she seemed to have time to chat with all of the passengers. When she learned that it was my first trip to Alaska and why I had come, she took an unusual interest in me. The stewardess was eager to answer all of my inquiring questions about south central Alaska living. At one point, well into the flight, she came to me with an invitation from the captain to visit the pilot's cabin. Sitting at the controls were two handsome, young men, who greeted me warmly. They looked very important surrounded by the navigational buttons, switches, levers, and dials above, below, and in front of them. All were within easy touch of their outstretched hands. I did so hope that they remembered how to use each. Their demeanor was casual and relaxed. Like the stewardess, they asked me lots of questions. "You should be a stewardess. We could use you," said the captain.

"Without a doubt you'll soon tire of working in a children's Home," added the co-captain. "If it doesn't work out, here is the name of the person you should see in Anchorage, and use our names as reference." I accepted the two business cards, but could hardly believe my ears. They were serious!

As I left the cabin, the stewardess told me that this particular airline (and I believe it was Pacific Northern Airlines) was in need of stewardesses. "We just think you have the right personality for the job." I thanked her very graciously but insisted that I was committed to the children's Home for three years. She repeated, "If it doesn't work out, come see us."

I returned to my seat and pondered the preposterous proposal. Within a short time, my train of thought was interrupted by the now familiar voice of the captain announcing over the intercom, "Since the airport for the city of Anchorage is under new construction, we will be landing at Elmendorf Air Force Base. Buses and taxies will be available to drive all passengers the short distance into town. Thank you for flying with us today. Enjoy your stay in Anchorage."

At the hotel I was pleased to hear the receptionist say, "Yes, we have your reservation." But then he added, "However, as you can see, we are under reconstruction, and there simply are not enough hotel rooms in town to accommodate all of the people who need them. As a result, we have had to put someone in your room. I hope you don't mind sharing a room with someone else?"

It didn't appear I had a choice. "Who is it?" I asked.

He quickly read a name from the register and then added, "She is a stewardess from one of the airlines. She isn't there now and will probably leave before you get up. If you are willing, here is your room key. It is a room with twin beds." I accepted the key. Sure enough in the room was the luggage of another occupant. It was a corner room on the first floor receiving the noise of two streets, 3rd and H. It was now the dinner hour, and I decided to dine in the hotel dining room.

The dining room was very pleasant, and I lingered at the table enjoying the view of Anchorage from the near-by window.

When I returned to my room, I saw that even though the drapes were closed, enough of the Alaskan bright summer night had crept in to allow me to be aware of the human beneath the covers in one of the twin beds. Gingerly, I walked across the floor, opened my suitcase and removed a gown. Picking up the overnight case, I quietly moved into the bathroom and closed the door. Once done with the nightly hygiene routine and dressed for bed, I turned the bathroom doorknob cautiously and stepped back into the room. The mass under the covers had not changed position, so I concluded that my roommate slept very soundly or perhaps feigned sleep to avoid introductions. I set the alarm and then glanced over at the head on the pillow of the other bed. All I could see was the top of the back of the head. It occurred to me that such tousled hair could belong to either a man *or* a woman. Adrenaline began to rush through my young body. Glancing around the room, I looked for clues that would reveal the true sex of the roommate. Ahhh, relief. A skirt and blouse were hanging over a chair, and a pair of women's shoes was placed neatly on the floor beneath them. It was proof enough to relax my tired mind, so I too fell into sleep.

When the alarm rang, my arm sprang forth to bring the rude intrusion to a halt, as though I had been programmed to protect the slumber in the other bed at all costs. I needn't have bothered. A quick glance around the room revealed that my roommate was gone . . . bag and baggage. I came to the realization that I had to have been in very deep sleep, not to have heard any movement at all. It was a nice feeling to know that the room was now all mine, and the only restraint on its use was time.

After a quick breakfast at the hotel, I was in a taxi headed toward the airport for small planes. Then minutes down the road, the taxi stopped at a small wooden building located between the dusty road and the airstrip. Once inside the building, I was assured that I was in the right place to catch a plane to Seward. The voices and faces were friendly, and indeed, they were expecting a Betty Jane Epps for a one-way trip to the lower peninsula town. The agent looked up from his book and seemed to eye my attire from head to toe, taking in the veiled hat, dress suit, gloves, and high heels. "Ever flown in a small plane before?" asked the smiling agent.

"No, I haven't. This should be an experience."

If he had wanted to comment on my wardrobe or the closed umbrella in my hand, he thought better of it. "You'll have a nice trip. It's a beautiful day."

In the small terminal, I glanced out one of the dusty windows. It was only then that the day's weather had registered. Well, of course, weather was important in flying, and I was probably lucky to do this virgin flight in a small plane on a sunny day.

Someone came in to collect the luggage and boxes nearby. "It will only be a few minutes. We'll load the luggage, and then you folks can board."

Two other passengers were seated against the wall. Their dress was much more casual, but the woman *was* wearing a skirt. The man was dressed in what I would soon learn to identify as an Alaskan tuxedo. It was the common attire of so many Alaskan men in the small towns when they dressed up . . . a grayish/green shirt-like jacket in a corded material and matching trousers. I followed these fellow passengers to the parked plane. About thirty-five feet away on the landing field was a shiny, silver, little plane with two propeller engines jutting out from the wings that rested atop the fuselage. On the side of the plane at the back of the wings was a small door that had been flipped up and rested like an open lid on top of the fuselage. Beyond this door were a few small windows indicating the passenger seats. We climbed in and filled the three empty seats and buckled our seat belts. We were surrounded by bags of mail and parcel post boxes. I had to assume my luggage was stashed somewhere behind and out of sight.

The roar of the motors preparing for take off seemed exaggerated inside the small cabin. Unfortunately, as we took off, the sound increased and was reduced only slightly during the remainder of the trip. To converse was to yell, so each passenger left the other to his or her private thoughts. The plane flew south along Turnagain Arm, an actual body of water from the Pacific Ocean, and then through mountain passes heading towards the east side of the Kenai Peninsula to the little harbor town on Resurrection Bay. Never had I been so close to such high mountains. Although it was nearing the end of summer, old patches of snow clung to the mountain tops, while low, lush, green growth grew as high up on the shale covering the sides of the mountains, as Mother Nature would allow. It was simply breath-taking to absorb nature's palette of a wide variety of shades of green, gray, and blue, with fluffy white clouds floating above for the finishing touch. Below, the alders and rough terrain looked uninviting for landing a plane in an emergency, but I decided to give the airlines the benefit of the doubt, and trust the pilot to get us to our destination. How very special I felt, as we flew for miles engulfed in such beauty. Suddenly I realized that soon I would be face to face with my young charges. Perhaps it would be wise to go over their names again. One of the staff, named Peggy, had sent me a letter with the names of the little boys, who would soon be in my care. I pulled the list from my purse and began to read. She had written that these were the youngest boys in the Home and all four and five years old. What strange sounds these last names in Eskimo, Athapascan, and Aleut languages! None like these were ever heard around Knoxville. For now I would concentrate on only the first names. I laid the list aside and tried to recite as many as I could quickly recall. I managed a few and stumbled. Oh, well, it will be easier when I can connect a name with a face, and that will be very, very soon, I thought.

Suddenly I became aware of the plane lowering altitude. The scenery was changing, and steep slopes were on both sides of the plane. What a strange sensation to be deep in the belly of the mountain range instead of high above it. Below I could see a gravel road and a rushing stream running along side. Houses began to appear here and there and occasionally, a car could be seen rolling along, leaving a cloud of dust on the unpaved highway. In the distance I saw a large body of water much larger than the mountain lakes we had flown over. That must be Resurrection Bay, I thought, and if it is, Seward must be on its shores somewhere. The houses became more numerous, and the plane flew even lower. It was hard to see what was ahead. As the plane came closer to the ground, the changing sights moved rapidly by the little side window. Suddenly I felt the wheels touch a graveled runway. A tiny hut was situated on the edge of the small airfield, and a cluster of people was standing near-by. I hoped that Mr. Matthews, the superintendent, was among them. There certainly were no cabs around. As the plane taxied toward the little hut, I began to make out the forms of little children. Why yes! They were little boys! Could they be mine? How nice that someone had brought them to meet me! Several adults were holding the hands of the children, and all eyes were glued to the approaching plane. Having brought the plane to a stop and the motors turned off, the pilot proceeded to open the plane door. Surely that was the last harsh noise to which my weary ears would be subjected. The man in the Alaskan tuxedo waited politely, while the female passengers gathered their things and moved towards the door to accept the outstretched hand of the assisting pilot. No sooner had I stepped from the plane, than a friendly lady approached saying, "You're Betty Jane Epps, I presume."

"Yes, I am."

"Well, I'm certainly happy to meet you," and she extended her hand for me to shake. Back home that was a polite custom for men only, but my mind quickly urged, if women shake hands here, then do it. The men folk in my family spoke negatively about limp hand shakes, so if I was to be forced into this masculine mode of greeting, I decided it should be done with gusto. I firmly grasped her hand and she responded in the same manner.

"Thank you. It's good to finally be here."

"I'm Ruth Matthews and this is my husband, Elwin. Mr. Matthews is the superintendent of Jesse Lee Home."

"Likewise," he smiled, and he too returned the firm grip. "We've brought almost all of the staff out to meet you, as well as the Nursery or D Boys, as we call them, because this is quite an event for us. Your coming completes our staff for the first time in many years." It sounded as though they really did need me. At this point, the rest of the gathering began to approach.

"Well, do I feel special! I'm delighted you all came, and these must be my boys. I've been practicing their names. Shall I try?"

"Uh, there's been a change, Betty Jane," began Mr. Matthews. "Three days ago I hired Mr. & Mrs. Bloom, who are now house parents for these younger boys." He might as well have hit me in the stomach. *Why did he do that? Did he get two employees for the price of one?* I was too stunned to give him the benefit of the doubt. He obviously had his reasons . . . whatever they were. I thought it best not to show disappointment. An elderly couple stepped forward following suit to warmly shake my hand. Each of them pulled the shy little boys a few steps in my direction and called out their names.

"This is Georgie. Sammy is under this big red hat somewhere," said Mr. Bloom, a big robust sort of fellow. He reminded me of a sea captain.

"This is Jack, this is Harry, and Tim, and peeping out behind me is Van," said Mrs. Bloom, wearing her white hair in a bun, looking very much the image of a matron in a children's Home, such as the one the

Rev. Fred McGinnis had described in Juneau. Each of the boys were bright eyed and curious. However, none of their soft-spoken greetings were audible.

"This is Miss Epps, boys. She's going to be the new housemother for the C Boys," said Mrs. Matthews.

So that's it, the C Boys. Which group are they? Thank goodness I still get to work with the children, I thought.

"The C boys are in school now, or we would have brought all eleven of them," she added. "They are first, second, and third graders. School started just today."

"I see," was my response. My thoughts clicked away. Well, the C Boys are still little. Perhaps I can handle that . . . I hope. Then my conscience scolded, 'No time for doubts. You *will* handle that, Betty. We've worked too hard and come too far. Accept the change. Adjust! Before I could formulate another thought . . .

"And this is Miss Bollinger. She is the housemother for the B Girls," said Ruth Matthews. And thus began a full introduction of each of the staff members.

"And here is Miss Gibson, she just returned from vacation recently. Pat is one of our deaconesses and the housemother for the little girls." Although there were no deaconesses in my church back home, I knew that title meant Pat was a special lady, who had felt the call of God to do work in the helping services. It also meant that she earned that title after successfully completing some courses of study and in this case, became a full-time missionary.

"And this is our housemother for the teenage girls, Peggy Dolliver, a U.S.-2."

"Yes, I'm the one who wrote to you," responded Peggy.

"Of course you are! I'm certainly glad to meet another U.S.-2!"

"We have another one still!" said Peggy. "But this is her day off. She said to tell you hello and that she will meet you later. I think she's gone into town today. Her name is Phyllis Dowling. She is from Massachusetts and is our relief housemother in the Girls Building."

"Now I think that you have met all of us. At least all that are here," concluded Mrs. Matthews, as she quickly looked over her brood. "We left Rachel Yokel behind. She is one of our deaconesses from the

Woman's Division. Rachel wanted more time to work on your room. You'll also meet Margo and Betty, who teach in the Seward School District down town, as well as being housemothers for our teenage boys. Dolores Morey has today off and she has the B Boys, the dorm above yours."

"Well, thank you all for coming to meet me. I wasn't quite sure how I would get from the airport to the Home. You all are a welcome sight."

"I see that we are going to have one problem," said Mr. Matthews with a grin, as he picked up a piece of luggage.

"What's that, Elwin?" asked his wife.

"We're going to have all of those C Boys talking in a southern accent before the year is out." The others responded with laughter.

"Oh, dear, is it that pronounced?" I asked.

"Never you mind, Betty Jane, we like it," said Mrs. Matthews, placing a reassuring hand on my arm. Elwin is just hoping your coming will take some of the teasing off of his Texas accent."

"Shall we go?" offered Mr. Matthews. "It is getting close to lunch time. We eat promptly at noon in the large dining room. Come, Betty Jane, we'll take you over in our car."

I took pleasure in hearing my first and second names used together. My family only used Betty Jane occasionally. I had signed my correspondence, "Betty Jane," and obviously, these folks had assumed that most southerners went by two names. It flowed through our conversation so naturally, I liked the sound and kept it.

The adults began to move towards the two vehicles. The little boys squealed and ran toward the truck. "Wait! You can't climb up there by yourselves," called Mrs.Bloom.

"Yes, I can!" yelled Sammy, who must have been the smallest of the bunch. He scampered up on the running board just as someone grabbed him and hoisted him into the bed of the truck. The other boys eagerly yelled for assistance.

"Doesn't anyone want to ride up front with Mr. Bloom and I?" asked Mrs. Bloom looking over the group in the bed of the truck."

"Not me! Not me!" came the consensus from the boys.

"You've had an ear ache," she said, pointing to one of the little boys. "Perhaps you had better ride up front with us on the way back."

"I'll pull my hat down over my ears like this. See?" responded the little boy, as he pulled a knit cap well below his ears. "Now, can I ride back here? Please, Miz Bloom. Can I? Can I, huh?"

Mrs. Bloom hesitated. "Well, as long as you keep that hat down over those ears."

"I will. I will!" he said and settled down into a corner of the truck between two jubilant peers. I could only conclude that riding in the back of the truck was a special treat.

"I'll see that he does," assured Peggy to Mrs. Bloom.

"So many of our children come to us with mastoiditis. We have to be careful with their ears," Mrs. Matthews informed me.

"I guess I'm not familiar with that term."

"It's an inner ear infection caused by a bacteria. As a result, the ears drain a lot."

All of the women were appropriately wearing slacks or jeans and warm tops. In comparison, I felt a little overdressed.

"I think this is your day off, Betty Jane," said Ruth.

"It's my day off, and I haven't even started to work?!"

"Yes, that's true," laughed Ruth Matthews. "But we may be making some changes shortly. However, for now this is your day off each week, and you'll get one Sunday off a month."

"I see." I turned to Mr. Matthews, "Did my trunk arrive?"

"You'll have to ask Peggy," he replied in a voice Peggy could hear. "She handles all of the large packages of mail."

"We've known you were coming for weeks! You have boxes, a trunk, and Rachel says lots of letters. The letters alone should take you all afternoon," yelled Peggy from the truck.

"Wonderful!" Once settled in the car, I asked the Matthews how long they had been at the Home.

"A few years ago the Woman's Division sent me up to be the farmer for Jesse Lee Home," began Mr. Matthews. "But when we got here, we saw there wasn't all that much farm to farm. So when Superintendent Green left, they needed someone to step into his place. I've been in that position since. We'll drive by and show you the garden. It's just right over here a ways. We grow lettuce, potatoes, carrots, radishes. Mostly root crops. They do well up here, even though the growing season is short."

"Cabbages get fantastically big," added Mrs. Matthews. "And of course strawberries do well. The kids love to pick strawberries. Here is our garden. There on the left side of the road." Mr. Matthews stopped beside a large, cultivated, flat area of about one and a half acres. The garden looked healthy and well attended.

"Do you grow most of your food then?"

The Jesse Lee Home garden. Photo from Rachel Yokel's collection.

"Oh no," Mr. Matthews quickly commented. "We are very limited as to what we can grow up here."

"Betty Jane, we order most of our food from Seattle, and it comes up on the boats," added Mrs. Matthews.

"But you do have grocery stores here?"

"Oh, yes. And we use the Seward groceries as we run out of items, but it is much more economical for us to order the bulk of our food and supplies from the States."

"And the boats come in the year around?"

"The barges and the freighters do. Seward is an ice free port. However, this will be the last season for the Alaska Steamship Company to carry passengers. The *Aleutian* will be coming within a few days with its last load of tourists," added Mr. Matthews.

The *Aleutian* once again filled my mind, and my memory flashed back to the ship and the Baranof Hotel in Juneau, and that preposterous letter of proposal. Immediately my focus was dwelling on what to do. Mr. Matthews had just said 'within a few days' . . . *I suppose I must prepare these folks for the inevitable knock on the door.* But this is hardly the time, I concluded. I will discuss that matter later. "Oh, the *Aleutian*! I got off of the *Aleutian* in Juneau, you know. It was a tremendous ship! The food was superb. What a shame to drop the passenger service."

"Our friend who works in the Seward office for Alaska Steamship says that the company is losing too much money," continued Elwin Matthews. "They simply can no longer afford to carry tourists." Instantly my mind questioned the economics of one waiter serving a table for 8 or 10 people for several consecutive days with only one person present. Was I guilty of perpetuating this sad financial picture?

"It's too bad. Some of our workers have come up or gone out on the Alaska Steamships and called it a trip of a life time," said Ruth.

"It is, believe me, and I really do appreciate the Woman's Division giving me the opportunity."

"Elwin and I had hoped to take it with our family, when we leave Alaska."

"You have children?"

"Yes, we have two boys living here with us and a daughter in the States."

The car pulled away from the site of the garden and continued down the gravel road. Shortly Mr. Matthews turned west and passed what appeared to be the town graveyard. Within minutes we were approaching the grounds of the Jesse Lee Home, and my heart skipped a beat. Suddenly, my thoughts were exclaiming, I'm here! I'm actually here! I'm twenty-two years old and suddenly the mother of eleven little boys. Am I really ready for this?

Chapter 7

BETTY JANE MEETS HER BOYS

M r. Matthews had taken a side road from the Seward Highway to a neat little white house that sat on the left at the end of the road. Just beyond, on the right, were three large buildings in a row that made up the Jesse Lee Home. Mr. Matthews parked beside the house. "That's the Jesse Lee Home over there, and this is the superintendent's house. We live here with our boys and two of the A Girls. Come in. We'll show you what it looks like," invited Mrs. Matthews.

"It's very nice and quite modern," I commented, as Mr. and Mrs. Matthews guided me through their house.

"Yes. Well, it was built some time after the other buildings. Someone, long before us, probably saw the need for the superintendent and family to be housed separately from the institution. We definitely need a place to get away from it all, because Elwin and I put in full days in the office and often tend to matters all over those three buildings. Plus we don't take all of our meals in the big dining room. We eat breakfast here and often dinner."

"I see and are you still the farmer, as well as the superintendent, Mr. Matthews?"

"No, Mr. Echols, our maintenance man, and the big boys tend the garden. That's about it for farming. I had big plans with my degree in agriculture to design a farm complete with more animals. That is not going to happen without a full time farmer on the staff. Guess my timing was wrong. When we arrived, the Jesse Lee Home needed a superintendent more than someone to develop a full farm."

"The Woman's Division said it would be temporary, until they could find some one to take the position of superintendent," added Ruth. "But they were so pleased with Elwin's administrative skills, he was asked to set the agricultural assignment aside and become the superintendent."

Mr. & Mrs. Matthews on steps of the superintendent's house. Photo from Rachel Yokel's collection.

"I'm curious. Is there a Men's Division?"

Mr. Matthews laughed, "No, not per se. There is a department of missions in the Methodist Church that is supported by all of its members, male and female, children and adults. As you know, the women have always been a strong force within the Methodist Church and are able financially to support their own mission program. Jesse Lee Home is one of the missions under the Woman's Division and is administered by a Board of Directors composed of women from all over the United States. Now they may hire men and even place them in administrative positions on their governing board, but by and large, all decisions made concerning the problems of each individual mission post are handled by the Woman's Division Board of Directors."

"And the financial support comes out of the Woman Societies of Christian Service in each Methodist church?"

"You got it!"

"You know, that's really something," I mused. "The women have done quite well, haven't they? According to the literature Peggy sent to me, Jesse Lee Home has been in existence for what . . . fifty some odd years? And I'm sure there must be other institutions under their wing with as much longevity."

"Sixty two years to be exact," contributed Mrs. Matthews. "The Home was started in 1890 out in the Aleutian Islands or 'the Chain,' as we call it. Jesse Lee Home was moved to Seward in 1925."

"You can see that date on one of the concrete posts on the center road entering the grounds. There! In front of the dining hall," said Mr. Matthews, as he pointed straight ahead to two pillars from the front windows of his living room.

"Yes, I see them."

"Rachel is going to wonder where we are! Let's take you to the Boys Building, so that you can meet Rachel and see your room. She is the relief housemother for the boys and is taking care of your boys today," stated Ruth Matthews.

Mr. Matthews added, "Actually Rachel is a lot more than that. She fills in for the superintendent when I am gone. She is our group worker, a field in which she was trained, but because we have been so short handed, Rachel has had to serve mostly as a housemother. She is a Methodist deaconess, as Ruth mentioned earlier, a full-time missionary, and an excellent staff person. You'll find her very helpful as you learn our routines."

"Sounds like I'm in good hands."

Back in the car Mr. Matthews commented, "You're right, Betty Jane. The women are to be commended for all of the mission work that they have begun, both in the Lower 48 and the foreign field, but there are lots of problems here. We keep waiting for more money, so that we can fix this and fix that. Like we told you, until today, we have had to make do with insufficient staff, while waiting for the Division to send us more."

"Elwin does hire locals, and sometimes people that the employment office in Anchorage send to us, but ours is not a nine to five job, and some of these folks don't stay with us very long." The car was about to pull up in front of the Boys Building. "There's your room to the left of the front door, and adjoining your room is the C Dorm," she said.

"On the first floor?"

"Yes," said the Matthews in unison.

My new domain was L shaped with my room being the small part of the L and the dorm jutting forward as the long portion.

"My gosh, those really are trees painted on the outside of the buildings! Why?" And thus began Mr. Matthews' story of camouflage during the war.

"You mean the war got into Seward?"

"No, no," continued Mr. Matthews. "But when the Japanese landed at Dutch Harbor (near the end of the Aleutian Chain), the kids were evacuated to Eklutna, just north of Anchorage and other places in Alaska. Some even went to the Lower 48 states until the war was over. The buildings at that time were glistening white and set between the mountains and Fort Raymond, a military base that was quickly set up in the fields bordering Jesse Lee Home on three sides. It was the coming of the Fort, more than anything, that led the superintendent to close the Home at that time."

"That move was about 1941," added Ruth. "With the kids gone, the military painted trees all over the buildings, hoping the three structures would blend in with the evergreens on the mountain side behind."

"So they are all evergreens. Pine? Cedar?"

"No, no. They are supposed to simulate spruce trees because that is what grows so profusely on the Kenai Peninsula. But around the back, behind the kitchen, some of the guys must have gotten tired of painting the limbs of spruce, because we have palm trees," Ruth chuckled.

"Really?" All three of us laughed. "Why haven't the trees been painted over?"

"That's one of the moneys we're waiting for," said Mr. Matthews shaking his head. "That bell is going to ring for lunch. We had better get Betty Jane inside," he urged.

We walked up the concrete steps and through the double French doors with the glass panes. Immediately to our right was Mrs. Bloom standing with her back in the doorway of her room and busily coaxing the young boys to get washed up for lunch.

"I'm cleaned, Miz Bloom, I'm clean," said one little boy, as he raised his hands for inspection.

Just for a moment, I harbored a pang of jealousy and resentment. What rotten luck to have this interloper appear on the scene and snatch the youngest boys from me. I had *so* wanted the care of the little boys.

"Yes, you are but Harry isn't. Harry, put that toy down and go get your hands washed," ordered Mrs. Bloom. Harry did as he was told. My well-prejudiced mind concluded that Mrs. Bloom was unnecessarily bossy.

"Those hands are not clean, Georgie. Did you use soap?"

"I cleaned 'em," insisted Georgie as he inspected his hands.

"Well, what's that?" she asked pointing to dirt still clinging to the palms of Georgie's hands. Aware of the presence of the Matthews and the new housemother, Mrs. Bloom greeted us with a hasty but friendly hello.

"That? Oh, that. That won't come off. Hi, Mr. Matthews. Hi, Mrs. Matthews. Hi, new C Boys' housemother," he said, grinning with a wide smile.

"Hi, Georgie, got those hands clean? Let me see them," requested Mr. Matthews.

"See, they're clean. I washed 'em. That won't come off," said Georgie pointing to telltale dirt.

"Georgie, my mother used to say, 'If at first you don't succeed, try, try again.' It looks like that is what you are going to have to do," he said.

Mrs. Bloom took Georgie by the hand and led him down the hall, "See, Georgie, even Mr. Matthews saw the dirt. Let's go try again."

Pulled by a force much larger than he, Georgie's feet cooperated, but his mouth insisted, as he stared at his one free hand, "They're clean. I cleaned 'em."

"You didn't even use soap," said another D Boy, as he passed Georgie and his housemother going into a bathroom. "I watched you."

"I did *so* use soap."

"You didn't!"

"I did too!"

"No, he didn't, Miz Bloom, I saw 'im."

"Never mind. Whether you used soap or not, they are not clean. We'll do it right this time."

Down the hall water could be heard flowing into a sink and Mrs. Bloom slapping a soapy mixture on Georgie's hands. Directly across from Mrs. Bloom's room and to our left was a single bathroom with an opened door. Apparently, Ruth saw that as a short-cut to my room, as she led us through that bathroom and then through the opened door on the opposite wall. "This is your bathroom, Betty Jane, and your room is here next to it," she said, not stopping until she reached the middle of the adjoining room. "Oh, there you are, Rachel. This is Betty Jane Epps, our new housemother for the C Boys."

A premature gray haired woman wearing glasses and a sparkling smile had stooped to pick up something from the floor. As she brought herself up to an erect position she said, "Hello, Betty Jane, pardon me if I don't shake hands, but they are full of the last bit of cleaning I was rushing to do before you got here."

"It's beautiful, Rachel. You did a good job," assured Ruth Matthews."

Rachel Yokel, Deaconess, Assistant to the superintendent, and temporary relief housemother in the Boys Building. Photo from Rachel Yokel's collection.

"It looks clean to me," I agreed. "Hello, Rachel."

"We're going to leave you two alone. Rachel, will you show Betty Jane how to find the dining room? You can bring her to my table for lunch, and we will place her at her own for dinner," requested Mr. Matthews.

"Sure. You bet I will," replied Rachel.

The Matthews left, and I stood facing this new personality with whom I would no doubt be working very closely. Rachel wore an air of confidence, and my first impression was that she was well in control of any situation.

"Mr. Bloom brought your bags in a short time ago, and there is mail that has been coming in for some time." She pointed to a large stack of envelopes on top of a desk.

"All of that is for me? Never in my life have I received so much mail!"

"Yes," Rachel smiled. "And over here is a trunk that Peggy sent over a few days back." My Dad's old familiar trunk was placed neatly against the wall near the door to the bathroom. The room had very little furniture. There was a single bed with its head under two tall windows, and the foot of the bed protruding out into the center of the room. Besides the desk, there were a couple of chairs and a chest of drawers against the opposite wall from the windows. To the right of the windows was a large round mirror hanging above a radiator. Two closets, one for clothing and one for supplies, were in the wall separating the bedroom from the adjoining dorm.

"We've had to scrounge around for furniture. With at last a full staff, there wasn't much left. I hope this will do. I'm sorry that we couldn't find a dresser. Maybe we could move the mirror above the desk, and let that double as a dresser until Mr. Bloom or Mr. Echols can find one."

Obviously, from my discussion with Mr. Matthews, there wasn't money to buy more. A possible solution popped into my head. "Suppose they could find a board to lay across the radiator? I could make a skirt to cover the radiator and use the board as a dressing table. Is there a sewing machine available?"

"You bet, several of them. In fact, you have a sewing room attached to the C Dorm. It's all yours. Come, I'll show you, and I'm sure they could find a board and even paint it for you. That's a good alternative,

Betty Jane. We do have some yardage in the big sewing room in the Girls Building. Mrs. Matthews will be happy to help you find something suitable."

I followed Rachel through the door leading out into the hall. I was happy to see there was another entrance to my room rather than the bathroom door Mrs. Matthews had led us through. The D Boys' bathroom was directly across, and Mrs. Bloom was still busy officiating the hand washing and combing hair as needed. On my left, a few steps away, was the entrance to the C Boys' dorm. Entering the little hallway, Rachel immediately led me into a room on the right. Two tall windows filled the room with light. In the center of the room was a pedal sewing machine. Half of the wall on the left was covered with storage space up to the ceiling, and the lower half was given to counters.

"This is where I mend the boys' pants and shirts," she informed me.

"I imagine there is a lot of that to do."

"Oh, yes. I usually set aside one full day a week and do nothing but mending."

"Every week?"

"Every week and then I don't always finish, but I hold it over until the next week and go on with other chores."

In one corner of the room was an ironing board with an electric iron unplugged sitting on its end. "And of course this is where you do the ironing," I observed.

"Yes, but I only iron their Sunday clothes. The boys are learning to iron their school shirts that are mostly cotton knit or flannel and also their good school jeans. On Sundays they wear white shirts and ties with nice slacks. If they are careful, they can usually wear the white shirts more than once before they have to be laundered. That way you don't have to starch and iron eleven shirts every week."

"And how are they at ironing?" I asked, assuming such skills were lacking in most juveniles.

"Surprisingly, most of them do a pretty good job. I usually stay here in the room to supervise and guide. They take turns as I call them in from play."

"Do they mind?"

"They mind being called in from play, but they don't mind ironing. Most of them look at it as learning a new skill, and I hear them boasting to the little girls in the dining room that they ironed their own shirts. It really doesn't take long. I always check to see if they made an effort to do a good job, before I let them go back to play. Floyd and Willy are new to the C Dorm, so they will need more direction than the others. They were just moved up from the D Dorm. They're first graders. Suddenly I felt as though stolen property had just been returned. So the Blooms didn't get all of my boys after all. It was as though the Blooms and I had made a compromise.

"I am impressed." I couldn't remember ironing when *I* was in the first grade, and certainly didn't remember seeing my two big brothers iron at any age.

"Come, I'll show you the dorm." I followed Rachel out of the sewing room into the little hallway. At the end of the short hall was an open doorway leading into a huge room. The room was well lighted on all three sides by many tall windows, just like the two in the sewing room. Eleven beds were placed around the room all tidily made with cotton spreads in like patterns of wide woven stripes on a beige background. Between every two beds was a chest of drawers, each containing four drawers.

"Each of the boys has two drawers and his own closet, as we loosely call them. They are located against this front wall as you can see, and each has a storage shelf for toys above the rod on which hopefully hangs his clothes. They keep their shoes and house slippers on the floor of the closet."

My attention was turned to the wall separating the sewing room from the dorm and the only wall uninterrupted by windows. On each side of the doorway could be seen the small closets. There were no doors, so the arrangement of the contents in each was open to the eyes of observers. On the floor of the closets were mostly house slippers in various stages of wear. They were placed neatly side-by-side, but I saw very few shoes.

"I don't see many shoes. Perhaps they are under the beds?"

"No, they are wearing them. Most of them have only one pair of shoes. That is one thing we are usually short of around here . . . money to buy shoes. People do send us used shoes, but in the few we get, it is hard to fit the boys comfortably into shoes that have been molded to someone else's feet."

"Of course. It would be." My eyes observed the floor. "The floor is certainly clean . . . not even a scuff mark."

"Oh, but there were! The boys and I cleaned the floor and waxed it last Saturday. I told them that you would be impressed at what good house-keepers they were, if they did a good job."

"I am. I am!"

Rachel glanced out the window. "I see the boys are coming home." A large group of boys in varying ages were running towards the Boys Building entrance. "All of the C Boys go to the former territorial school called Bay View. The boundary was just changed, and now this school is in the Seward School District. It is just back beyond the Girls Building. Did the Matthews point it out to you on the way over?"

"No. I missed it. The boys walk to school then?"

"Yes. All of our elementary students do. Those in junior high and high school go downtown on the Jesse Lee bus. The men on the staff drive them back and forth. Here comes the bus now." A yellow bus was clumsily passing the superintendent's house and coming into its parking place by the Girls Building at the far end of the property.

"They come home for lunch?"

"Yes, it isn't too far. It's more economical and more convenient than having our cook, Mrs.Echols, prepare a sack lunch for all of them. Shall we go? The bell will ring shortly, and you might want to wash up."

"Yes, I should change or get out of this hat at least."

"Oh, no, don't do that. Let the boys see you as you are. They will like that. They don't get to see the staff all dressed up in their nice clothes very often."

Rachel's request surprised me. *Well, why not do as she suggests, if she thinks that is important?*

As we reentered the hallway, two little boys came rushing up to Rachel. "Miz Yokel, doz boys are splashing water in the bathroom!" accused one of them.

"What boys?"

"Dem boys, dare!" he remarked, as two more boys came out of a door beyond the D Boys' bathroom.

"Yeah, Ben and Carl," responded the other one.

"Ben and Carl! Are you playing with water in the C Boys' bathroom?" she asked accusingly.

"I didn't do nothing!" said one of them.

"Me neither. It was those guys in there." He turned and pointed an accusing finger into the doorway.

Rachel left immediately with the two small accusers following close behind. Within moments the culprits were apprehended, and Rachel could be heard saying, "That's enough of that. Miss Epps, your new housemother, has just arrived. You have just enough time to come out into the hall and meet her before the bell rings for lunch."

"Has she?" asked one wide eyed little boy.

"Where is she?" asked another.

"What does she look like?" came a third question.

"Come out into the hall and see for yourself."

At that, a scramble of young boys pushed their way into the hallway and looked in my direction.

"Is that her? Hi!" said one with a big smile.

"Yes," said Rachel, separating the group in order to get through the bathroom door. "Come down the hall, and I will introduce you."

With wide grins the small throng of boys followed Rachel. "Miss Epps, these are the C Boys . . . or some of them. This is Willy and Floyd, the two first graders. This is Carl, Ben, and Alvin. And that is Max bringing up the rear." A bevy of curious little native boys and one Caucasian made me the center of their attention.

"Well, hello! I'm happy to meet you all."

Numerous greetings came at the same time. "Hi. Hello. Hi! Hi. Hello." One giggled and said, "I'm pleased to meet 'cha." The others laughed.

"Miss Epps is from Tennessee."

"Tennessee! Where is that?" asked one.

"Tennessee is a long way from here," I replied, not knowing how far their knowledge of geography extended.

"They talk like *that* in Tennessee?" asked one. More giggles.

"Tennessee is in the southern United States. Yes, they talk like Miss Epps . . . in a southern accent."

"FunNEEEEE," he responded. He obviously found the sound strange.

"Better get your hands washed for lunch, if you haven't already," said Rachel to the boys.

"I did! When dat guy splashed me," said Willy, still upset and feeling offended.

"Well, 'dat guy' isn't going to splash anyone anymore, are you, Alvin?" demanded Rachel of the little Caucasian boy with the mischievous grin. "I'll see to that." She took the little boy's hand and marched him to the bathroom. Alvin looked back over his shoulder with a shy look of guilt registering on his face, while his teasing eyes searched mine for a reaction.

Uh, oh. Is this one going to give me trouble? The group quickly dispersed and our eye contact was broken. Some of the boys followed Rachel, while others ran into the dorm.

Willy and Floyd stayed behind with me. I assumed these were the two that had been recently moved up to the C Dorm.

"What did she say your name was?" asked Floyd with a big friendly grin.

"Epps, Miss Epps. Can you say that?" I asked.

"Funny name," he laughed.

"Mis Sepps!" they both responded. I smiled, assuming that was probably as close as they were going to get. And actually, it was.

"How come you talk like dat?" asked Willy.

My urge was to reply, 'And how come you talk like that?' However, in my new role as a mother figure, I knew such a response would be inappropriate. "Everyone talks this way where I come from."

"Tennessee?"

"Yes."

"Geeeeeeeeee! FunNEEEEEEE!" I was yet to discover that I would be hearing that expression over and over again.

"I'm from Nome," announced Floyd, determined to get into the conversation.

"That's a long way too from here, isn't it?" I asked.

"Yeah." Floyd let that thought settle in his head and then added, as he pointed at Willy, "But *he's* not from Nome."

"I'm from Unga," said Willy, making the announcement before Floyd had a chance. With those facts quickly disposed of Willy moved on to the important stuff. "How long *you* gonna stay?"

His question took me by surprise. He had emphasized the '*you*' implying that the previous housemothers hadn't stayed very long. Apparently, it wasn't common knowledge among the children that a U.S.-2 stays three years in Alaska. "Why . . . three years," I said, searching his big, sparkling, brown eyes for a response. Suddenly the realization hit me that the care of this little native boy was all mine, and maybe we wouldn't be ready to part with each other after three years. "Well, maybe five," I added on impulse.

"Five years! Wow!" beamed Willy walking away as though he had just received the best news in the world. The loud noise of the ringing bell jarred me from the warm glow I was enjoying from Willy's response. A scurry of rapidly moving feet could be heard all around . . . down the hall, from stairs above and more boys coming through the front door. Suddenly boys were everywhere in all ages, shapes, and sizes.

Leaving the C Boys' bathroom, Rachel called in my direction, "Betty Jane, if you are ready, we'll go over to the dining room now."

"Oops! I still haven't washed the travel off of my hands. Just give me a minute. I'll step in here." I quickly retraced my steps to the bathroom that Mrs. Matthews had pointed out on the route to my room, when we came through the front door. Hands cleaned I joined Rachel in the hall, and we moved with the thundering herd making way for the arcade door. Above it all, I heard Mrs. Bloom warning her charges, who were trying to keep up with the older boys, "Remember, we do not run in the arcade!" Then raising her voice even higher, "Georgie! Do you hear me?" Georgie brought his fast paced steps to a halt and indignantly turned around to challenge his accuser.

"Not me! I'm not running. This is not running." The oncoming flow of traffic had to quickly maneuver around him to avoid knocking him down. By this time, Mrs. Bloom had caught up with Georgie and had taken him by the hand.

"Well, you were just about to move into a run."

"No sir, not me," he continued quickly, as she escorted him into the dining room.

Bigger boys passing by the scene seemed amused at the scolding. Georgie was aware of their pleasure. He didn't like it, and the expression on his face told them so.

Like the Boys Building, the dining room jutted forward to the front of the campus. I observed that the formation of the many dining tables was that of a rectangle, matting the room like a picture frame. As in the C Dorm, on all but one of the four ivory painted walls were many tall windows, making the room very light and cheery. Green plants and flowers lined the widest of the three walls. Large flowered drapes hung at the windows. Opposite the wall with the plants was the kitchen with a serving counter and a door on either side of the counters separating the two large rooms. Food was on the tables, and five to six children were standing at each table with a staff person.

Rachel escorted me to Mr. Matthews' table and then quickly walked nearby to sit and officiate at her own. One child was asked to move to another place, so that I could be seated beside Mr. Matthews. The

Children eating in the JLH dining room. Photo from Rachel Yokel's collection.

youngster gave me a curious look and did as he was told. The table seating was mixed both in age and sex.

"Every few months or so we change the table seating to give the kids a chance to eat and visit with others," Mr. Matthews commented.

Everybody stayed on their feet until Mr. Matthews clinked his silverware on a glass to get their attention. Immediately the room fell quiet, and all eyes were on the superintendent. At this point I was introduced, and he gave me a moment to extend a greeting. He then gave a blessing. This being brief, they immediately sat down, and the staff person at each table began serving the food.

There was a large container of soup with a large soup ladle waiting to be used to distribute the contents to all six at the table. Mr. Matthews began the serving, as a metal pitcher of milk was poured for each child. "You can have coffee if you like," offered Mr. Matthews. "The big boys bring it around to the staff."

"Thank you, but I believe I'll have milk with the hot soup."

"Well, let me warn you, our milk is not fresh. It's powdered milk shipped out of Seattle, and if the boys do a good job of mixing it, it's okay. Otherwise the milk may taste a little different to you."

"I've never tasted powdered milk. I'll give it a try," I said, pouring the white beverage into the hard plasticware cup. It certainly *looked* like milk. I ventured a sip. To my surprise the temperature of the milk was cool, not cold, and in place of a rich, fresh milk flavor, my palate had to endure a watered down, powdery, artificial taste of something akin to milk. I looked around the table to see how the children were accepting this impostor in the milk pitcher. Several already had white mustaches on their upper lips, and little tongues were trying to erase them. One would have thought they had just partaken of something very refreshing. Obviously, their taste buds had not been pampered with rich, fresh milk.

"Mr. Matthews, she doesn't want her soup. Can I have hers?" asked a little girl.

"May I," he corrected.

The little girl smiled and ducked her head in slight embarrassment, as she glanced momentarily in my direction to see if I had been aware of her misuse of grammar.

I responded with a smile, as Mr. Matthews patiently told the child, "No. Neva needs to eat her soup, so she can go back to school this afternoon and be a good student. You finish what you have, and you can probably have seconds. Did everybody get carrot slices?" Several heads bobbed affirmatively. "Well, I didn't get the bread or the butter."

Obviously, the bread and the butter were stalled in their passage around the table at *my* place. Mr. Matthews turned to me and said softly, "'Tennessee,' will you pass me the bread and butter?" His teasing manner softened the no-no I had just committed by not keeping all of the food moving around the table until everyone was served.

"I'm sorry, here it is," I said quickly, slipping a slice onto my own plate before passing him the stack of white bread slices. I hoped the buttered bread and of course the soup would surely help me get the awful milk down and save face with the children. I couldn't imagine many of them getting by with leaving any food uneaten. I looked down at the hot bowl of soup still steaming. "My compliments to the cook to be able to serve this many people and still have the soup piping hot. How many people are in here?"

"About one hundred when we are all here. Mrs. Echols has lots of help with the older boys and girls. When she has it ready they carry it to the tables, and the bell rings immediately. As you could probably see, nobody wastes any time getting to the dining room."

"No, not even Georgie," I laughed.

"Running in the arcade again, huh?"

"Almost, but Mrs. Bloom slowed him down."

"The housemothers in the Girls Building have their share of 'Georgies' too. We'd probably shake that mountain behind the building loose, if we let them all come to meals at their chosen pace."

"I don't like moose," announced Neva with an expression to match her pronouncement.

"Did you find some moose in that soup, Neva?" he asked.

"Yes, and it's yucky."

"No it isn't. That's good for you. You eat it." Reluctantly, Neva went back to her soup.

"Does it taste like beef?" I asked picking up my soup spoon.

"Depends on how it is fixed. Some folks think it does. Try it."

The soup looked like a combination of vegetables and little chunks of meat. Tiny ringlets of fat floated here and there. *Was that from fatty tissue in the moose?* Unfortunately, its appearance reminded me of a soup I hadn't seen or thought of for years . . . nor wanted to. It was known unappreciatively as "dishwater soup" and called thus by every elementary student in the hot lunch program at Mynders School in Knoxville. But I realized this was jumping at conclusions and prejudicing myself before I had even taken the first spoon full. I glanced around the table at the children, and all but Neva were emptying their bowls with appetites appearing to be satisfied. I tried the soup. Again my taste buds rebelled! It was undoubtedly the worst soup I had ever had in my life. Not even Mynders soup could touch it.

"What do you think?" Mr. Matthews asked.

"I think it tastes . . . different. It certainly doesn't taste like beef."

"It's probably the wild taste that you aren't used to."

Not wanting to go public yet on my distaste for Mrs. Echol's culinary efforts, I said, "Perhaps. Uh, well, it *is* different." I looked across the table to see how Neva was doing. Muttered at a low audible, I heard her final critique, "It's yukky." But like a trooper she was eating it, and I knew that too was to be my destiny, albeit without the luxury of even one little "yuk" (at least none uttered aloud). I kept eyeing the plain lime Jell-O that appeared non-threatening to one's palate, and assured myself there would be no negative gastronomic surprises there. I was right, and forever grateful to Mrs. Echols for not tampering with the Jell-O.

"We're lucky, Tennessee," said Mr. Matthews, getting to his feet to dismiss the group. "The Fish and Wildlife Department give us hundreds of pounds of moose every year. It sure helps on the meat budget."

"Poor Neva," was all I could comment. And to myself, *not to mention 'Mis Sepps.'*

Chapter 8

BETTY JANE LEARNS
THE ROPES...ALMOST

Lunch was over. Mr. Matthews clinked his knife against the glass. All conversation in the big dining room abruptly stopped, and remained so until he uttered the word, "Dismissed." The contrast in sound that followed was rather startling to say the least. Suddenly the room was filled with the noise of one hundred bodies hurriedly moving chairs and feet scurrying in all directions. The big kids began to clear the tables, gathering silverware, dishes, and carrying leftovers to the kitchen. It was like a big wave of energy spilling in all directions, and then flowing back into the room to wipe the tables clean, sweep any crumbs that may have fallen from the tables, and rearrange the chairs. As they completed their assigned chores, each child asked for permission to leave the dining room. The staff person assigned to dining room duty quickly inspected the work, and if the job was acceptable, permission was granted. Once again the arcades were filled with energy, as kids hurriedly returned to their respective dorms to do whatever was necessary to get back to school for the afternoon.

During all of this hubbub, I was introduced to the cook, Mrs. Echols. She was definitely among the older members of the staff; her long gray hair was pulled back into a bun, and her full figured body was attired in a cotton dress and apron. We spoke only briefly with a polite exchange, for it was obvious, Mrs. Echols was distracted by her charges coming with questions and complaints of somebody not doing something right. And of course, there was the pressure of time to finish all the dining room and kitchen chores, before the big yellow bus left to take the big kids back to town.

After lunch Ruth Matthews gave me a tour of the area where the girls resided. Leaving the dining room, I followed Ruth into the arcade that lead to the big building on the right of the campus. As we entered the hall of the Girls Building, we immediately turned left into the laundry sorting room, and I was told how the housemothers gather one day a week to sort the clean clothing that is washed at the Sanatorium. "You will be assigned a specific day to do the nicer clothing of the C Boys and your personal laundry."

"In here? Where are the laundry units?"

"Oh, no. Not here. We have a washing machine in the basement of this building. Rachel will take you down there but for now, let me show you the staff kitchen, where we often gather for tea after sorting laundry." I followed her into the adjoining room. "Some of the staff bake birthday cakes here."

"Instead of using the regular kitchen? Why is that?"

"Our kitchen appliances are made for preparing large quantities of food. When a birthday is celebrated in an individual dorm, a single ten or twelve inch cake is best prepared here."

"I see."

"This room is also available for *your* use on your days off, if you don't wish to eat in the main dining room. Incidentally, the kids are not allowed in here without a staff person."

We left the little kitchen and stepped across the hall into a sewing room, that contained large tables for spreading out material. A few bolts of cloth were on the shelves, and a few peddle sewing machines were in the room. A young housemother was sewing a seam on a dress.

"We teach the big girls to sew in here," remarked Ruth.

"But I'm not one of them. I'm Peggy, the U.S.-2 that met you at the airport," said the staff member at the machine.

"Of course you are! Are *you* making a dress?"

"No. I'm just mending a dress for one of my A Girls."

"Do the A Girls make all of their clothes?"

"No, thank goodness. They'd have very few dresses if I had to teach them. But I do know have to sew up a ripped seam."

"At one time, many years ago, the older girls *did* make their own clothes," offered Ruth. "But not anymore. Our budget covers *some* new clothing. Mostly clothes are donated to us, and some girls arrive with their own. We put out a request list with sizes from time to time that is sent to all of the Methodist churches in the Lower 48. All of these boxes that you see on the tables are filled with clothing waiting to be opened.

Ruth Matthews, wife of the superintendent, opening boxes with Peggy Dolliver, A Girls' housemother and a U.S.-2. Photo from Rachel Yokel's collection.

"And they won't have to wait much longer, Ruth. As soon as I finish sewing this seam, I'll get back to that job," said Peggy.

"That's okay, Peggy. I know you'll get to it when you can." And to me she said, "Some of the clothes in the boxes are new, and some are used. Peggy and I open the boxes and store the items in the attic of this building. We have a section designated just for brand new items, both for girls and boys. The house parents go up there from time to time and choose whatever is needed, but the children are not allowed up there. I'll show you the attic sometime, but first, let's finish touring this floor."

I said goodbye to Peggy and we stepped out into the hall and moved forward toward the front door of the building. An office was located right by the front door. I noted that anyone entering the Jesse Lee Home would most likely happen upon office staff immediately. It was a typical office of the time with desks, typewriter, filing cabinets, and shelves for storing records and books. It was a large room and appeared well used with work in progress on the two desks. Mr. Matthews sat at one desk, and the other was no doubt for the secretary.

"Hello, 'Tennessee,' he greeted me warmly. "Ruth giving you the five dollar tour?"

"It feels like the ten dollar tour. She's a great guide!"

"Not quite," said Ruth. "I see Elwin has a stack of mail on my desk to handle soon, and that means I may have to cut this tour short. In fact, why don't you take her down the hall and show her the guest suite, Elwin. I have a matter I must tend to right away."

"Sure. Come, 'Tennessee,' just follow me down the hall."

Further down the hall and just to the right of the entrance to the building was the set of rooms for guests.

"From time to time, we house traveling missionaries from the mission at Unga, out in the Aleutian Islands, and administrators, who come for on-site visits from the Woman's Division in New York. You'll see these guests show up at my table in the dining room from time to time."

Pat Gibson, Deaconess, and housemother with her C Girls. Photo from Rachel Yokel's collection.

I noticed the guest suite had much nicer furnishings than the odds and ends in my room, with a very nicely decorated bedroom and bath.

"Also, when not otherwise occupied, this living room is used for weekly staff meetings. The staff in this building often entertain their visitors here as well."

"And is there a room for entertaining guests in the Boys Building?"

"No, I'm afraid not." Suddenly there was a quiet pause in our conversation. Then he smiled and said, "You expecting visitors, 'Tennessee'?" Instantly I was reminded of the waiter on the ship, and wondered if this might be a good time to tell him all about that fiasco. No, I decided to wait.

"Just curious. I'm not expecting visitors."

"Let's go across the hall, and I'll let Miss Gibson show you her C Dorm. These are the youngest girls." He knocked on her door saying, "Unlike the Boys Building, we have no preschool age dorm for the girls, because we only have one little girl in that age range." The door was opened promptly by a little black haired girl with big brown eyes. "And here she is now! Hello, Leona, is Miss Gibson around?"

"Yes, I'll go get her." And she dashed away.

"So we placed Leona with our youngest girls, who are in the first, second, and third grades. Leona will go to school next year. "

I marveled at how well he seemed to know the names of all the children. Soon we were greeted by Pat Gibson with Leona in tow.

"Come in," Pat said. "Are you giving our new housemother a tour, Mr. Matthews?"

"Yes, but I'm about to turn her over to you. Ruth has shown her the first floor but not your dorm. Maybe afterwards, you can take her up to the second floor to see the A and B Dorms."

"Why I'd be happy to. Come in, Betty Jane. Just let me turn off the iron. I've been ironing dresses."

Mr. Matthews turned to leave saying, "Thanks, Pat, and show 'Tennessee' how to get back to the Boys Building when you are through."

"I will," she assured him.

Leona closed the door and I watched Pat unplug the iron on the ironing board in her room. "Ironing ruffled dresses is so time consuming, I try to iron while the other girls are in school."

"That's *my* dress Miss Gibson is ironing," said Leona proudly.

"And it appears to be a very pretty dress too," I remarked.

"Our large dormitory room is much like the C Boys' dorm with beds and chests of drawers lined around the walls. Here it is. As you can see it is connected to my room." A bathroom with multiple toilet stalls was near-by. Each bed was neatly made, and I noticed the bedspreads were similar to those on my boys' beds.

"Your girls are good housekeepers. This room is very neat."

"We are!" Leona reassured me.

"Sometimes," replied Pat smiling. "But they have to be reminded."

"Not me, huh, Miss Gibson?"

"Yes, Leona, you are usually a good housekeeper. Now we'll go out into the hall from the door in my room. You may remember there was a set of stairs leading up to the 2nd floor right outside my door."

Upstairs a similar set up was found for the intermediate-aged girls in upper elementary school. However, the older A Girls were privileged to share rooms with a single roommate or two. It was very quiet with all of these girls back in school for the afternoon, and neither of their house-mothers was around.

"Now I'll take you up to our attic."

I was amazed at all of the clothes and new toys that were waiting mostly for birthdays, Christmas, and special needs. It was like a big country store without cash registers. "Peggy has done an excellent job of organizing these items, so that housemothers can easily find what is needed," said Pat.

"Yes, I can see that."

"I bet the mail has arrived! Mr. Echols or Mr. Bloom have usually picked it up at the down town post office by now. The staff comes to the office to get their mail after lunch. Shall we go see? Mail time is always a high point in our days here at Jesse Lee. Then I'll get you to the arcade, so you can return to the Boys Building." Then Pat paused, "But you are welcome to stay and watch me iron, and visit with Leona and I. There are several more dresses dampened and rolled up waiting to be ironed, and I do *so* want to get that done before the girls get home from school."

"Another time perhaps. I haven't had time to unpack. Thank you for the tour."

We made our way to the office and sure enough, the mail had arrived. There in a cubby hole labeled, "Betty Jane Epps," were *more* letters. I was *delighted*. Ruth looked up from reading a letter at her desk. "Back from the tour, Betty Jane? I see Elwin turned you over to Pat. Thanks, Pat."

With Pat's direction, I found my way to the arcade, and soon returned to the boys' domain and my room. At last I could take off my hat and relax. Before unpacking, I couldn't resist going through that big stack of mail and enjoying the sight of personal letters from family and friends! It was, without a doubt, a euphoric feeling to once again connect with all of those caring people, who were interested in this new phase of my life. I felt very special indeed!

I unpacked and found storage space for all of my belongings. The second closet had supplies for the boys, as well as candy. Rachel had taped a note to the candy saying she was in the habit of putting sweets on their beds before they came home from school. "They look forward to this welcome snack," she had written. "The fact that it is Christmas candy out of season doesn't alter their appreciation in the least."

I closed the door of that closet and looked in the big round mirror hanging over the radiator. I saw the reflection of a young, somewhat naive twenty-two year old about to become the mother of eleven little boys. *Can I do this? I'm not even an experienced baby sitter. Sure, I've taken care of my sister's young children once or twice, but that's about it.* I was always too busy with assignments at the University to do more. Well, it was too late for doubts, and I knew a lot of people were counting on me. I had no intention of letting anyone down. I walked to the window and looked out. There before me was this great expanse of land leading down to the Resurrection Bay with a back drop of the dramatically beautiful Mount Alice. Even though it was August, snow still clung to the higher elevations. Houses could be seen far down the road leading into town. The lagoon road split a body of water, and occasional traffic could be seen bumping along this road. I felt blessed to have such a view, and even more blessed to have this experience of caring for these young boys.

Suddenly there was a knock on the door. "It's me, Betty Jane. Rachel. I thought you might like a tour of this building."

"Sure, come on in," I replied, opening the door for Rachel.

Rachel remained in the hall saying, "I just saw Ruth, and she said you had been given a tour of the Girls Building. Is this a good time? If not, I can come back later."

"This is a perfect time. Let's do it." I stepped out into the hall, and closed the door behind me.

We moved across the hall as Rachel began, "As you know, the C Boys and the D Boys have the first floor." As we entered a short hallway, just to the left of the D Boys' bathroom, she continued, "Here are two large empty rooms, that were once used as a third dorm at some time in the past twenty-seven years. Now they are used as playrooms."

"Are these two playrooms specifically for the C Boys?"

"Yes, but on Saturdays, after they have done the weekly cleaning, the boys gather around a large table in the smaller room, and polish their shoes for church attendance the next day. I guide them through this process and approve each boy's efforts, before he is released to play for the rest of the day."

I observed that both rooms had linoleum floors. The bigger room had large, tall windows, as were in all of the other large dorm rooms, but no furniture at all. The large table for shoe polishing was the exception in the smaller room.

"Now let's go down to the other end of the first floor towards the arcade, and I'll show you the rooms used by the D Boys. These rooms are a little smaller, and one is used as a work room for their housemother, so she can be in close proximity to the boys at all times." I followed Rachel into the D Boys' dorm.

"Hi, Mrs. Bloom," said Rachel, "I'm just showing Betty Jane around the Boys Building."

"Well, I'm afraid we are a mess right now. Be careful and don't slip and fall over one of their construction toys. Sammy! I thought I told you to pick up these toys ten minutes ago! We have guests, and they can hardly get into the room, because you didn't pick up these toys." A little boy ran into the room.

"Huh? Me?"

"Yes, you. Pick up these toys." Sammy looked at the unexpected guests shyly, and dutifully began picking up the toys. He placed them into a box.

"It's okay, Mrs. Bloom. We can step around them. Do you mind if I show Betty Jane where the little boys sleep?"

"Why no. Come on in. I'll show you the dorm room myself." Rachel and I followed Mrs. Bloom into an adjacent room. It was not quite as big as the C Boys' dorm, but had beds in a similar arrangement all around the walls with chests of drawers in between the beds. "As you can see, the rooms in this dorm are in the back of the building, while my housemother's suite is across the hall at the front of the building. I don't like that. My hearing isn't so good, and I feel I am just too far away from these little boys at night."

"So if they get into mischief at night, you're not apt to hear them," chuckled Rachel. "That could be an advantage, Mrs.Bloom."

"Well, they don't get by with much with Mr. Bloom around. His hearing is better than mine. He'll nudge me in the night, if he hears one of them. "Course we've had a knock or two on the door in the middle of the night."

"It's been my experience with these little boys that they are quite willing to tattle on the other, if the opportunity arises," offered Rachel.

"Oh, yes. We learned that from the very first day. The first night I brought them all into my room for a story before bed time, and had to listen to all of the grievances before I could begin. I thought we'd never get to the story."

"That sounds like them," said Rachel. "Thank you for letting me show Betty Jane the D dorm. I'll take her upstairs now."

"You are very welcome. Come back anytime."

As we moved into the hall, Rachel continued, "Stairs are located at both ends of the hall leading up to the 2nd floor. We'll take these stairs outside the D Boys' dorm. At the top of the stairs, we stopped at the door to a suite of rooms on the left. "This is Miss Morey's room, but she is off today, so I can't introduce you to her. However, her table is next to yours in the dining room, so you'll meet her in the morning. We proceeded down the hall. "Next to Miss Morey's room is John Street. He is one of our maintenance men here for the summer only. He'll be returning to college in Texas soon. He is a friend of the Matthews, and Elwin brought him up to lend Mr. Echols a hand." We continued down the hall to the end. "Here on the left is the B Boys' dorm. As you can see, it is located directly above the dorm of the C Boys." We stepped inside the dormitory room, moving to the windows on our left, and I could readily see the front steps to the Boys Building and my room below.

"Oh, my!" I commented. "They *do* have a view. They can see for miles around."

"In the summer time when darkness is almost nil, the light sleepers hear every sound below these windows, and keep tabs on the social life of all of the single staff members. The next day one is apt to hear them announce their observations of the night (imaginary or otherwise), while grinning and teasing a wide-eyed, unsuspecting staff person."

"Really? Well, I'll consider that fair warning, but since I don't know any of the local gentry, I don't see that as an immediate problem."

Rachel smiled, "Well, you never know. Phyllis Dowling, in the Girls Building, has asked that Ruth assign your day off with her. She goes to the square dance club every week, and I'm sure she'll introduce you to the local gentry there, if you like square dancing."

"Well, that's sounds like fun. I used to square dance with my Dad back home."

"Phyllis loves it. Couldn't interest any of the rest of us to go with her. She'll be delighted to know that you are interested."

We left the B Boys' dorm and stepped across the hall to the gymnasium. Rachel opened the door and I exclaimed, "Oh, my! A real gym with hard wood floors and all! And I see basketball hoops mounted at both ends of the gym!"

"After the dinner hour, this end of the building is filled with noise."

"Basketball?"

"Sometimes. The Methodist minister, Charles Malin, comes up in the evening once a week, and coaches a basketball team that competes in the community. Other nights the kids roller skate here. Sometimes it's just a big place to run off excess energy. Each dorm gets an assigned time.

They can use the gym any way they wish. The big boys usually practice for the basketball games."

Back down the hall from the gym on our left was the B Boys' bathroom with shower stalls and multiple sinks and toilets. Just beyond and across from Miss Morey's living area was the chapel. A simple worship center was set up on a raised platform at the front of the large room. A very nice, black, grand piano was on the right near the platform. "Let's step inside, and I'll show you something that denotes a little of our history." So we did. "Look over your head up in the back corner of the chapel near the ceiling and you'll see a window which was once used as a viewing area. Sick children on the third floor above, most often with terminal tuberculosis, could see and feel a part of services in the chapel."

"But none of the present kids have tuberculosis, do they?"

"No. However, when Jesse Lee Home was moved from Unalaska to Seward in 1925, the top floor in this building was used as a hospital but not now. Quite a few of the children suffered from tuberculosis and had to be quarantined from the rest. As the story goes, one very sick patient expressed a wish that she could see the children in the chapel singing, as well as hear the sound of their voices coming through the wall. One of the maintenance men at the time cut the hole in the wall and placed a window there as a birthday present for this child."

"What a nice story. What happens to children with tuberculosis today?"

"TB patients are sent to the San here in Seward. Fortunately, a Native Service hospital is presently being built in Anchorage to care for such patients. Our third floor is simply a dormitory for the A Boys now."

"Is the chapel still used for services?"

"Not on a regular basis. Once the Methodist church was built in Seward, there was no longer a need to maintain a church within the Jesse Lee Home. So the big yellow bus takes us back and forth to town every Sunday." She paused. "Now, let's go back to the other end of the hall, and climb the last flight of stairs. I'll show you the third floor, where the A Boys reside with their house parents. Betty Boyd and Margo DeWild somehow manage to teach school in town, and be the house parents to these teenage boys as well."

"That sounds like a challenge."

"Indeed it is. They divvy up the responsibilities, and it's working out for all concerned right now."

"That's impressive."

At the top of the stairs Rachel said, "Like the A Girls, these older boys have the luxury of several rooms and assigned roommates." We peered into a few of the rooms. Rachel said, "Well, Betty Jane, this pretty much completes our tour. I'll let you get back to what you were doing, and I'll be back with you tomorrow. It's Saturday, our housecleaning day. I'll show you our routines."

"I'll look forward to that, and thank you very much for the tour."

Since it was my day off, I spent the rest of the afternoon answering some of the many letters, knowing full well that mail time was going to be my contact with the world outside of Jesse Lee. As I composed each letter, I was transferred back in space and time to the last moments I had spent with that particular individual. Through pen and paper, I became far removed from Alaska, until the loud clang of the dinner bell jarred me back into the present reality. I quickly washed up. Soon I was among the thundering footsteps once again moving through the arcade.

At the evening meal, I discovered that my assigned table was near the entrance to the kitchen, next to Dolores Morey's table. However, Rachel sat in Dolores' place, as was expected of her, since she was the relief housemother. Remembering the procedure at Mr. Matthew's table at lunch time, I picked up the pitcher of powdered milk, and poured it into the cups of the five young children, who sat quietly observing this new housemother. Since house parents could be selective in what beverage they drank with the meal, I knew none would be questioning the fact that I did not pour myself the powdered milk. I asked the children to tell me their names, and with shy smiles they responded. Then the food was passed around. They all ate heartily and talked very little. I observed that each had good manners, and appeared adjusted to institutional dining. No one complained about the slices of pork roast, boiled potatoes, and green beans. Perhaps most of them had already concluded that I was just one of many parent figures to pass in and out of their lives. As I panned the faces around the table, I decided that if they survived my inexperience, I would probably learn far more from them, than they from me.

After dinner Rachel caught Betty Boyd and Margo Dewild, as they were passing by the table leaving the dining room. "Margo! Betty! I want you to meet our new housemother." Introductions were made and I observed that Margo was a tall Amazon beauty and Betty Boyd had an intelligent face that said she was on top of any situation. Conversation was brief, because the A Boys were approaching them with one concern after the other.

In reply Betty demanded, "Not until you've done your homework."

"I did it, Miss Boyd! I did it!"

"Then I want to check it." At that the two young women excused themselves and moved out of the dining room.

Rachel then turned her attention to me. "Betty Jane, about tomorrow's cleaning . . . the boys know what their Saturday jobs are. They keep the same jobs for a month or so. Your job is to check each one before they are free to play. I'll be down first thing in the morning. Some of them like to get started before breakfast. I usually let them."

"How early do they get up?"

"The wake-up bell rings at 6:15 a.m., but you may hear some of them up before then."

"Even on the weekends?"

"Every day of the week."

I thought to myself, *uh oh, can I handle this? I am not a morning person.* But alas, this was the beginning of my new real world. I would have to get used to it.

The next morning the wake-up bell was loud and shocking to a sleeping body, unaccustomed to rising at such an early hour. From the immediate sound of voices and quickly moving feet in the hallway, I surmised that these young boys did not have that problem. Remembering that Rachel would be on the scene bright and early, I quickly jumped into some comfortable clothes, threw some water on my face, and combed my hair. Having noticed the day before that the other staff members did not wear make-up, I skipped the lipstick.

When I opened my door leading into the hallway, I saw that Rachel had already arrived and was urging the boys to get ready for breakfast. Some of them had been permitted to start their regular Saturday cleaning chores, hoping to get them out of the way, as soon as possible, and start playing. Others took a more casual attitude about the assigned chores, and playfully dawdled around the sinks, as they washed up for breakfast. This mix of personalities clashed from time to time, and confrontations were immediately reported to Miss Yokel. Rachel reminded them, "Miss Epps is now in charge. You need to take your concerns to her." At that point, I had appeared on the scene. "Oh, here she is now."

"Good morning," I said. "Is there a problem?" Not knowing if the new command would be sympathetic to their cause, their eyes dropped to the floor, their mouths repeated something almost inaudible, and they sheepishly turned and walked away. It seemed almost within seconds a loud bell sounded throughout the halls, and the pattern of a thundering herd moving towards the dining room began once again. Rachel quickly turned to check the dorm to make sure all of the boys were on their way. I wondered at the necessity of her action, for obviously, no one could miss the sound of that loud bell, which must have resounded into the ears of the wild life for miles around. But I was to learn . . . that was Rachel, always making sure. As we walked through the arcade together, I noticed that the D Boys would attempt to tell Rachel of some injustice they had suffered at the hands of one of their mischievous peers. Raising her voice over the den of noisy footsteps and voices, she would say, "Tell your housemother. Tell Mrs. Bloom! Not me. I'm not your housemother today."

"I did!" would often be the come back.

"One of the drawbacks of being a relief house parent," she said to me. "You're looked at as the next in command to their housemother with the authority to bring doom down on the offender."

"And I suspect if the matter wasn't settled to their satisfaction, and you're standing near-by, there is always a chance you might see things differently," I ventured.

"You've got the picture," she laughingly added. "But I try not to interfere in a house parent's decision."

After breakfast once again the big dining room was emptied, but not before I got a chance to meet Miss Morey. Dolores Morey was blonde and near my height of 5'3".

"Welcome to Jesse Lee, Betty Jane. I'm Dolores. We've been expecting you. Sorry I didn't meet your plane yesterday, but I had an engagement in town. It was my day off."

"Yes, that's what they told me."

"I live above you on the second floor with the B Boys."

"Rachel gave me a tour of the Boys Building yesterday and showed me where you reside. I'm certainly happy to meet you."

"If I can help you in anyway, let me know." Immediately some of her charges appeared with a question or two. I observed that some of the intermediate boys at ages ten, eleven, and twelve were as tall or taller than Dolores, but from their body language I could tell that Dolores commanded the same respect as someone towering over them eight feet tall. It was obvious that she took a no nonsense approach with these boys.

I left Dolores to deal with her boys and hurried back to the C Boys' domain. As I approached the bathroom, I saw that those assigned to clean that room were playing around, so I went in to investigate. The boys were using very little cleanser and removing very little soil, so I picked up the can to show them how much to use. "As a child, this is the way my mother taught me to get a sink clean."

"Wow, that much?!" they exclaimed.

"Well, you want to get it clean, don't you?"

"Okay!" they yelled with glee and passed the cleanser can for a more generous offering.

I went on my way to check on others. Down the hall one of the boys was sweeping with a large push broom that dwarfed his height. In the big dorm room, a couple of boys were manning large dust mops that accumulated little piles of dust and debris brought into the dorm on the shoes of eleven boys during the past week. Rachel was standing there praising their efforts, and the boys produced big smiles.

"I think you are showing Miss Epps what good house cleaners you can be."

C Boys sweeping their dorm floor.

At that point someone came in claiming that Willy was not cleaning the glass French doors at the entrance to the building on *both* sides, 'like he was supposed to.'

"I'll go," I said to Rachel.

I found the youngest member of the C Dorm wiping each small glass plate on the door from the inside. His accuser said, "See, he's just doing it on the *inside* . . . not the outside."

"You can't tell me what to do," said Willy. "You're not my boss, Carl."

It looked like a power struggle. "Well," said Carl, as he picked up a broom and headed through the door to sweep the front steps, "That was my job last month, and *I* had to do both sides."

"I'm sure Willy intends to do the outside, when he has finished the inside. Won't you do that, Willy?" I asked.

"Dat boy always tryin' to tell me what to do. He not my boss."

"He *said* he wasn't going to *do* the outside. That's what he *said*," chimed in Carl.

C Boy cleaning glass panes inside the front door of the Boys Building.

"Of course he is, and I'll be back to check how well he has done *both* sides when he is through. Why don't you get started on the front steps now, Carl?"

At that point I heard Rachel's raised voice yelling from the bathroom, "Who told you to use that much cleanser? Why that's enough for a year! That's wasteful! Cleanser costs money."

"She told us to," said one of the boys softly.

"Who told you to?" snapped Rachel.

"Mis Sepps," said another one.

I felt like a little kid who had just done a giant 'no-no'. Rachel stumbled in her reply. "Well . . . that's too much. I'll talk to Miss Epps."

At that point my brain stored this incident away in my memory in a tight little box reserved for low self-esteem. I was convinced that I had not lived up to Rachel's standards on my very first day of work. Now, *I* was to be reprimanded. This would be awkward, to say the least. It hadn't occurred to me that the boys probably doubled the amount of cleanser demonstrated. I allowed the guilt to rest totally on *my* shoulders. I decided *I* was at fault. The door to my bathroom was standing open, so I quickly escaped into my private quarters momentarily with thoughts clashing in my head. *What is wrong with me? Of course it is important to be frugal in a place like this. I am guilty of extravagance! I am wasting the Mission Board's hard sought money being too generous with the cleanser. What to do? I can't spend the whole morning dodging Rachel. I'll have to face her sometime and get it over with. How embarrassing! Of course I have no choice. Eventually, I must return to the hall and take the consequences. Oh dear!*

Chapter 9

A PORCUPINE, A CONFRONTATION AND A BOX OF CHOCOLATES

I very carefully looked around as I opened the bathroom door that led into the hallway. Rachel was nowhere to be seen, and I breathed a sigh of relief. Suddenly the front door on my right opened, and in came a six foot tall, curly brown haired young man.

"There you are! Hi, I'm John Street, and you are the new housemother."

"Yes, I guess I am," I replied, looking up at the fellow built like a big lumber jack.

"I understand you have Sunday off. Me too. If you'd like I . . . "

At that moment Dolores appeared, having come down the stairs with several of her boys behind her. "Oh, hi, John! Have you come to rescue us from the porcupine that is eating the wooden foundation out from under this building?"

"Mr. Echols told me about it. Has anybody actually seen it?" responded John.

"Yeah!" said one of the B Boys. "I seen it. It's under the C Boys' dorm chewin' on the wood."

"Wanna show it to me?" asked John.

"Yeah, come on. I'll show ya. It's on the far side of the building," said the B Boy.

"Excuse me, Betty Jane. I'll stop by later." He followed the boy down to the end of the hall toward a door that exited to the outside.

I looked at Dolores. "Porcupine?"

"Yes, the boys say one has been chewing on the foundation for several days now."

"Have you seen it?" I asked.

"No. Let's go have a look." We moved down the hall, followed by a collection of boys from both the B and C dorms. Dolores turned abruptly and said to the group, "Don't go out there making noise, you'll scare it away, and none of us will see it."

"I've never seen a porcupine," I said to Dolores.

"Neither have I." One of the B Boys opened the door at the end of the hall and saw John on all fours on the ground peering under the building.

"Can you see it?" asked the boy.

"Yeah, he's under there alright . . . chewing away," replied John. Immediately all of the boys spread out along the side of the building and fell to the ground on their knees with eyes searching in the dim light underneath.

"I don't see it." "There it is!" "Where?" "Over there!" "By that black thing!" "I see it," came the cries of the boys.

Dolores and I walked over to John and joined the others on hands and knees. "Where is it, John?" asked Dolores. John pointed to the large porcupine.

"Yes, I can see it. Well, look at that!" Dolores got up off of her knees. "He's there all right. Plain as day. Can you see it, Betty Jane?"

"Come over here to the other side of me, Betty Jane. You can see it well here," suggested John.

I came to a standing position and then moved down to the left of John. I knelt again and saw a wild beast in a crouched position with dark eyes staring back at me from about twenty feet away. "Oh my! It sure is. What are you going to do? Catch it?" I asked John.

John grinned, "Don't think I can do that. Might have to shoot it."

"You got a gun, John?" asked a wide eyed boy.

"No, but Mr. Matthews does."

"Well, I'll leave this wild animal safari to you, John. I have to go check on the other B Boys and their Saturday work. All you B Boys back to work!"

"Awww, Miss Morey. I bet we could catch it, if we tried," said one.

"No, that's John's work. Not yours. Back upstairs."

Suddenly a young C Boy came through the now opened door. "Mis Sepps, Miss Yokel is looking for you."

I got up off of my hands and knees. Uh oh, I thought, I know what's coming. I might as well face Rachel and get it over with. "Tell her I'll be right there," I replied. As I turned to follow the boy, John called after me.

"Hey, Betty Jane! Know how to cook porcupine?"

" 'Fraid not!"

"All southern girls know how to fry chicken, don't they?"

"Well, yes, I can fry chicken," or I assumed I could. How hard could it be?

" 'Then let's have fried porcupine!"

At that moment Rachel appeared as I reached the door. "Oh, there you are, Betty Jane. Mr. Echols is here with a board, and Ruth has brought over a bolt of material for you to look at."

"Okay, Rachel. I'm coming. We were just looking at the porcupine under the building."

"Porcupine?"

"Did you not hear about the porcupine?" I asked.

"No." Seeing John still on his hands and knees she called, "Is it still there, John?"

"It's here. Come have a look while he's still alive."

"Oh, my! You sound like the great white hunter!" She immediately went to John and knelt on all fours to his left.

I went into the building relieved that the confrontation with Rachel was not yet happening. Down the hall I saw Ruth and an elderly, thin man standing outside my door. If this was Mr. Echols, he certainly was smaller in stature than his wife. When I arrived Ruth said, "Hello, Betty Jane, this is Mr. Echols. He wants to build you a dresser."

"How do you do, Mr. Echols? I guess this is the first time we've had a chance to meet." I extended my hand to the man in what I assumed was the expected Alaskan greeting.

"Yes," he said, shaking my hand. "I've been pretty busy, but they tell me you need a dressing table and here it is. Don't look like much yet, but maybe with that cloth Mrs. Matthews has in her hands and your sewing, we can make something of it."

"Wonderful. Come on into the room." The two followed me into my room, and Mr. Echols laid the board on top of the radiator located under the mirror on the wall next to the bed.

"Just wanted to see if this board is long enough. Hmmm. I'll just take an inch or two off of it, and then I believe it will work. You want me to paint it?"

"That would make it more serviceable," chimed in Ruth. "Think you can find some enamel paint somewhere, Mr. Echols?"

"We don't have much choice in color, but maybe we could buy a color Miss Epps would like," he responded. Immediately the cleanser extravagance came to my mind, and I certainly didn't want to be known as the new staff member who made unnecessary demands on the budget.

"Whatever you have in enamel paint will be fine," I quickly replied.

"Have any thing in one of the colors I have in this bolt of material?" Ruth asked Mr. Echols. The material was cotton with a small green and black pattern on a white background. "Betty Jane, this is one of the few materials we have on hand now that would supply enough material for a skirt to go around the radiator. What do you think?" she asked.

"That material is fine. I can work with that."

"I know we have enough *black* enamel to cover the board," offered Mr. Echols. "Tell you what, I'll paint the board and let it dry before I attach it to the wall. That okay with you?"

"That will be fine. Thank you. I won't attempt to make the skirt until the board is in place."

"Betty Jane, I'll just leave this bolt of material in your sewing room, so it will be there when you are ready for it. You can return what is left to the sewing room in the Girls Building. Oh, by the way, beginning next week you'll be having your day off with Phyllis on Fridays instead of Pat. That was Phyllis' request. I hope that is okay with you."

"Certainly. That's fine."

"Phyllis said she'd come over from the Girls Building to discuss some plans with you. Think that includes the Square Dance Club on Thursday nights. She's eager to get with you."

"I have Thursday night off?"

"Yes. We arrange the schedules so that you get the night off before your one day off each week."

"Sounds like fun. Maybe I'll see her at lunch."

"Speaking of lunch," said Ruth glancing at her watch, "it's getting close. I have some stuff to finish in the office beforehand. I'd better run."

"Thank you both. It will be good to give the room a little creative touch." Both Mr. Echols and Ruth turned to leave and go their separate ways, just as Rachel appeared at the door.

"Betty Jane, you wouldn't believe the amount of cleanser the boys were using in the bathroom this morning. They insisted you said it was okay." Immediately, my face turned beet red. As a red head, embarrassment always lit up my face like a neon sign, and there was no hiding it. "If I let them use that much cleanser, there would soon be none left."

I was just too embarrassed to defend myself and wanted the conversation over as soon as possible. "I'm sorry. I'll watch that."

But Rachel wasn't through. "I told the boys that cleanser costs money. They shouldn't be wasteful. Living in an institution, we have to be mindful of such things. We can't just let them use as much as they like. When I went in there, the place was a mess with cleanser on the floor as well as the sinks."

"Oh dear, I . . . "

Suddenly one of the C Boys appeared at the door. "Can we polish the shoes now? I'm ready."

"No, Chuck. It's almost time for the lunch bell to ring. We'll do it after lunch," responded Rachel. "Oops! I'm sorry, Betty Jane. That should be your decision. It usually works better after lunch. I just jumped in there due to habit. Ask Miss Epps, Chuck."

"After lunch will be fine," I replied quickly and certainly relieved to have a change of subject.

During lunch I allowed my mind to ponder Rachel breaking her policy of never interfering in how a houseparent handled a child. I guessed the offense was so great that it merited her stepping over the line on the cleanser. That thought landed in the pit of my stomach like a thud. I did so hope Rachel would not share this incident with the Matthews.

I considered myself conscientious, and my overwhelming desire to please Rachel and look good on this very first day with the C Boys was simply not happening. Whether Rachel would hold the conflict over the cleanser as a judgement against me was yet to be seen. However, being young and inexperienced, I was convinced this would be a stumbling block in being completely comfortable around Rachel from that point on. I would simply have to learn to live with the awful fact.

Dolores broke that unpleasant train of thought, as she commented from the adjoining table, "Think the great white hunter has successfully stalked and saved us from the dreaded jaws of the porcupine?"

It was the comic relief I needed. "I don't know," I chuckled. "Think he'll shoot it?"

"Oh, yeah! When he gets back to Texas, I can hear him now. 'Sure I went hunting in the wilds of Alaska. Shot my first porcupine and saved a three story building from collapsing.' " Dolores laughed enjoying her own witty nature. I gratefully obliged with a hearty laugh, somewhat surprised at how quickly that little bit of humor raised me up out of the funk the cleanser had caused.

C Boys polishing shoes.

After lunch, Rachel, the C Boys, and I all gathered around the big table in the smaller playroom to clean shoes.

"Here, first let me spread this big tablecloth, so we don't get shoe polish on the table," said Rachel.

"We sure got it on the table cloth," said one of the boys. I observed a very stained cloth with big splotches of brown and black being very pronounced on the faded light blue background.

"I don't got a rag!" announced Ben.

"All in good time," responded Rachel, as she took rags and shoe polish out of a box and distributed them around the table. The boys were wearing house slippers, and each was carrying a single pair of shoes. The cans of shoe polish were opened, and the boys began to furiously rub the dark polish into the leather of their shoes. "Brian, let me look at your shoes." Brian handed Rachel his pair of shoes, and she examined them closely. She then turned to me saying, "We have to buy special shoes for Brian."

"He's pigeon-toed," chimed in one of the other boys.

"Yeah, he's got pigeons on his toes," giggled another one. The others laughed.

"You shud up," demanded Brian under his breath.

"All right, that's enough of that," said Rachel. "Brian was born with a deformity in his feet that makes his toes turn inward when he walks. That's nothing to make light of," she scolded. "I believe you can get a few more months wear out of these shoes, Brian. You're taking good care of them."

"Are the special shoes helping?" I asked.

"Well, we think so, don't we, Brian?"

Brian muttered, "I dunno." He was still miffed at the boys for laughing at him.

"I'm through, Miss Yokel," said Chuck. "Check mine," and he handed her his pair of shoes. I watched to see how high Rachel's expectations were in the task of cleaning and polishing shoes.

"Let's see, Chuck. You usually do a good job. Uh oh, here's a spot on the back of this one above the heel that you need to work on."

"Where? Let me see." She handed the shoes back to him pointing at the designated area. "Okay. Please pass that brown shoe polish back to me, Ben," said Chuck. Ben did as he was asked.

"This gives Miss Epps a chance to see what condition your shoes are in, so she can let Mr. Matthews know when one of you needs new shoes."

"I need new shoes!" "Me too!" "Look at this, Miss Epps." "Awww, that's nuthin'." "Look at mine," came the comments of the boys simultaneously.

"Are there new shoes in the attic?" I asked.

"No. We don't ask for new shoes but *money* for shoes instead. It's better to take the kids down to the local shoe store and fit them individually. It's a priority on the list of needs, and it doesn't arrive in abundance. Oh, a few used shoes come in unsolicited, but once a shoe has molded to someone else's foot, it doesn't adjust well to another's growing foot. We keep those used shoes in the basement of this building. I'll show you sometime. We only use them in an emergency."

By now several boys were saying, "Check mine." "I'm through!" "Me too!" "Look at mine!"

As I examined each pair, I noted that I was looking at an array of shoes in varying stages of wear. Those who had done a good job of smearing polish all over the shoes were dismissed to play until the polish dried. "Is there a shoe repair shop in town?" I asked of Rachel.

"We use the shoe repair shop at the Rehabilitation Center at the San. The Center is trying to train patients who are about to move back into the community, with skills that could allow them to earn a living. That shop helps us out some, but in a very limited way. Not many of the patients show an interest in learning the skill. Mr. Matthews told me that at one time, an A Boy displayed a gift for repairing leather, and that boy kept many of the shoes in good repair. That enabled the boys to get a little more life out of their shoes, but that was a long time ago. The boy has moved on, and no one stepped up to take his place." Pretty soon the room was vacated, and eleven pairs of shoes sat on the table drying from newly applied shoe polish. "We can call them back in about thirty minutes. We'll give them polishing rags to shine their shoes. They get a kick out of the new shine on their shoes, and it becomes a competition."

"You, and no doubt others, have trained them well. They are good at cleaning, whether it is the dorm or their shoes. I'm impressed."

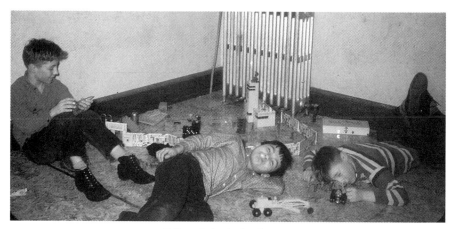

C Boys playing in the playroom.

At that point, Phyllis appeared on the scene displaying her jolly personality. "Oh, there you are! One of the C Boys said I'd find you in here. Observing the eleven pairs of just polished shoes, she commented, "Hmmm, shoe polishing time, huh? Think I could slip a pair of mine in here, Rachel?"

"Give it a try, Phyllis, but I can't guarantee we can get one of the boys to leave his play long enough to make it worth your while."

"No, I probably would have to bribe them with something. A second dessert at the table maybe?" Phyliss chuckled.

At that point, Dolores walked into the room. "Hey, if you bribe with chocolate, *I* might even do it for you."

And I added, "Or I!"

"So you're a 'chocoholic' too?" laughed Dolores. "Don't know if this town is big enough for the two of us, Betty Jane."

"Surely you haven't *consumed all of* the chocolate in Seward yet, Dolores," said Rachel teasingly.

"I would if I could. You better believe it!" she laughed.

"I have some chocolates you can have. I don't want them," said Rachel seriously.

Almost in unison we three responded, "You don't want them?!"

"No," then she lowered her voice and looked all around the room. "Please don't tell this. I certainly don't want Mrs. Bloom to know this happened, but Mr. Bloom knocked on my door last night and handed me a box of chocolates."

"He didn't! What? Really! Why?" came the responses of the three of us.

"I don't know. I told him I couldn't accept the chocolates, but he insisted that he thought I deserved them. 'I admire your work here,' he said. 'I just want you to have them.' "

"Is Mrs. Bloom in on this gift?" asked Phyllis.

"No, that's the problem. He asked me not to tell Mrs. Bloom, that she might not understand. He refused to take the box of chocolates back."

"Rachel, looks like Mr. Bloom has a crush on you," said Dolores in amusement.

"Well, be that as it may, I can't accept chocolates from a married man, and I told him so."

"Where are the chocolates now?" asked Dolores.

"They are up in my room. I'm going to write him a note and give them back. What would you do?"

"Well, in my case, I'd threaten to tell Mrs. Bloom if he didn't appear at my door at least once a week with the chocolates," said Dolores. We laughed.

"Seriously, what would you do?" Rachel asked.

"Stop the presses! This will make a great story to put in the Kueuit!" announced Phyllis. Again there was laughter.

"What is the Kew-it?" I asked.

"Oh, you don't know about our newsletter, Betty Jane," said Phyllis. "I'll have to give you a copy to read. In fact, one of the things I came over for was to ask you to write up your first impressions of Jesse Lee Home. I'm the editor. We usually ask the new staff to submit something. You don't have to do it for this issue, but I wanted you to be thinking about it for the next."

"No offense, Betty Jane, but I think Rachel's story would be juicier," said Dolores, refusing to let the humor escape from the situation.

"Hmmm, but how can we get it by the censorship of the Matthews?" asked Phyllis, supporting Dolores' sense of humor.

"Oh no, I'm not ready to share this with the Matthews. If Mr. Bloom doesn't discourage easily, I may have to resort to that. At this point, this is all very confidential, you three."

"Mums the word, Rachel, unless I run out of material for the Kueuit," chuckled Phyllis.

"Who gets this Kew-it?" I asked. "By the way, how do you spell that?"

"K-u-e-u-i-t," spelled Phyllis. "Just about every Methodist Church in the Lower 48 gets the Kueuit, plus the New York Mission office, and anybody who has ever made some contribution to the Home. Oh, it has wide readership!" said Phyllis.

"Including all of the dorms in Jesse Lee Home," added Dolores.

"Rachel, you need to join Betty Jane and I at the Square Dance Club on Thursday nights. That's the place to meet available bachelors. Pick yourself up a beau, and that will scare Mr. Bloom away," said Phyllis.

"Hope it doesn't come to that," she responded.

"I came down to ask if it is my turn to check on the A Boys tonight, Rachel? I understand that Betty Boyd and Margo have some function at the school tonight," added Dolores.

"Yes, it is your turn," said Rachel. "I think some of the boys will go with them but not all of them. I have a prior commitment or I'd do it, Dolores."

"Okay, that's what I was afraid of," replied Dolores. "You handle those big boys much better than I. Most of them tower over my five feet and one half inch and can be a bit intimidating at times. But I'll do it. Later!" she added and left the room.

At that moment Chuck appeared on the scene. "Are the shoes ready to polish?" he asked of no one in particular.

"I bet they are. Go call the other boys, and I'll pass out the shine cloths," acknowledged Rachel. Chuck turned immediately and left the room to do what he was told.

"Betty Jane, I must apologize that the Kueuit has kept me so busy meeting this deadline, that I haven't had time to do much more than nod in your direction in the dining room," offered Phyllis.

"That's all right. I'm not offended."

"I'm so pleased Mrs. Matthews gave you Thursday nights off with me."

"Yes, she told me that this morning, and also that we'd have Fridays off together. I'm looking forward to you showing me the sights around Seward."

"You're in good hands, Betty Jane. Phyllis has been here for two years and knows a lot of people in town."

Suddenly the sound of running feet announced that the C Boys were returning to the shoe cleaning table. "Here they come. I'd better grab the shine cloths." Rachel reached her hand into a box underneath the table and pulled out a bunch of individual cloths and tossed them on to the middle of the table.

As each of the C Boys arrived at the table, arms reached for a cloth with voices exclaiming, "Give me one." "That's mine!" "Hey! I had that first!" etc.

"I'd better get out of here," said Phyllis. "I'll talk to you later, Betty Jane. And Rachel, *give* it back to him! What a jerk!"

"I agree," said Rachel.

* * *

That night Dolores had just finished reading to the B Boys, and all appeared quiet in the dorm. Her next job had yet to begin. She disliked those nights when Rachel couldn't carry out her duties as relief house-parent. That sometimes meant Dolores was in charge of two dorms. The little boys weren't so bad, but the A Boys could be down right frightful at times. Oh, well, somehow she'd get through it. She had some time yet. The B Boys had gone to bed at 8:00 p.m., and the older boys weren't scheduled to bed down until 9:00. It *was* important that the boys get to bed on time, especially on school nights. Of course tomorrow would be Sunday and not a school day. However, the entire Home would be expected to be up as usual at 6:15 a.m., and ready to go to Sunday School and church shortly after breakfast. She decided to go to her room. She would read a new book she had started until it was time to deal with the A Boys upstairs. Walking back to her room, Dolores was reminded of the time she filled in for Rachel during the day, as well as the evening, in supervising the big boys. She made a point of climbing the stairs several times during that day to check on them. On one of those trips, she was surprised to see a huge, live duck nesting in a box in the hallway. Intuitively, she just knew neither of their two housemothers was aware of this addition to the top floor. Did she really want to deal with that? She decided on the course of least resistance, and left the matter up to their regular house parents to settle. As tall teenagers on their way to manhood (ages twelve-eighteen), their facial expressions concealed inner thoughts that made them appear unapproachable at times. Yet they could be very solicitous to their little brothers and sisters. This was Dolores' observation at the many birthday celebrations, when brothers and sisters were included in the individual dorm's party for the honoree. Most had siblings living there, and it was one of the few times that they gathered as a family unit.

At 8:45 p.m. Dolores closed the book she was reading. With a sigh she brought her five feet and one-half inch to a standing position and readied herself to put the A Boys to bed. As she passed the B Boys' dorm, she was grateful for the quiet that relieved her of having to deal with problems in two dorms at the same time. She was almost in the middle of the flight of stairs to the third floor, when she looked up and saw one of the bigger A Boys standing on the top landing, taking a John Wayne stance with a BB gun across his arms. In his best threatening, yet calm John Wayne voice, he demanded, "What d'ya want, little Missy." Of course he knew full well what her answer would be.

"It's time for the A Boys to get ready for bed."

Still in the John Wayne character, he replied, "You're too little to be a housemother."

If he was looking for a power struggle, she decided his statement was probably correct. Since she had no firearm, she'd have to rely on the power of words to reach this would-be cowboy. She straightened her posture to strengthen her composure in the role of authority and simply stated, "Please give them that message." Dolores then turned on her heels and calmly walked away, never divulging to him how intimidating this scene had been. Each dorm had its own unique challenges, but she never quite expected that. A short time later, things were pretty quiet on the top floor, so Dolores assumed 'John Wayne' had delivered her message.

* * *

Downstairs I was enjoying the peace and quiet of my room. I had just written three letters to friends back home. Suddenly a soft knock was heard at the door. When I opened the door, there was John Street with a big grin on his face. "Remember me?" he asked.

"Hello, John." I wasn't sure it was appropriate to invite him into my room, so we remained at the door. "How could I forget? They call you the great white hunter around here."

"That's what I want to talk to you about. If I shoot the porcupine and skin it, will you fry it?"

"Who is going to eat it?"

"You and me. Will you do it?"

"Well, we'd need a frying pan, grease, and a stove to cook it on. And some flour too."

"Don't worry about that. I'll get all of that stuff. We'll do it some night after you've put the boys to bed."

"John, I don't have a night off soon."

"No problem. I'll bring over a hot plate, and you can cook it here. If the boys are in bed, you'd be free to do that, wouldn't you?"

I pondered if that would be breaking any rules. Having a single man in my room might provoke suggestive thinking, but it occurred to me the sewing room might work. "Okay, but let's use the sewing room. Do you fry porcupine like you fry chicken? John, I'm not sure I know how to do this."

"Sure. Why not? Let's give it a try."

I smiled at the thought, "Okay. When are you going to shoot it?"

"Sometime when the boys aren't around. It might bother some of the little ones. I'll let you know as soon as I've done it."

"Okay. You do that."

It was an awkward moment. John didn't seem to want to leave, but I hadn't invited him in. However, I held my ground. I simply couldn't risk another 'no-no' on my very first day of work. There was no lounge in the Boys Building to entertain a guest. There was only the front steps of the building, but that wouldn't do. Certainly no privacy there with the daylight extending into the summer night. *Should I attempt to continue this conversation or . . .*

"Well, just wanted to make sure you'd fry the beast, if I shot it. I won't keep you from what you were doing."

Ahhhh, the perfect out. I said to John, "Yes, I was writing letters."

Chapter 10

FRIED PORCUPINE AND SQUARE DANCING

After breakfast one morning, Rachel reminded me that it was my turn in the basement laundry over in the Girls Building. "After the boys go off to school, gather their dirty dress shirts together and your personal laundry, and I'll be glad to show you how our washing machine works."

"Thanks, I'll do that." Once my last boy had brushed his teeth and was out the door, I went to the C dorm. I sorted through the white shirts hanging in the individual open closets to see which needed washing.

Suddenly Rachel appeared saying, "Only take the shirts that are really dirty, because it is time consuming to wash and iron eleven white shirts every week. Each freshly laundered cotton shirt has to be dampened and then rolled up into a ball. I then leave the shirts to set for a while to absorb all of the moisture before ironing. It's the only way to remove all of the wrinkles. A few of the boys manage to wear a shirt twice before it needs laundering but unfortunately . . . not many."

I took a second look at the soiled white shirts I'd collected and said, "I believe these are the dirtiest. I'll go and grab my own personal laundry bag, and I'll be ready."

In the basement of the Girls Building, I followed Rachel into a huge, dark room with no windows. She turned on the lights, but the basement walls remained very dark, and many plumbing pipes were exposed overhead.

In comparison to the rest of Jesse Lee, it felt like a dungeon. A single family-sized white washing machine stood in a corner near a couple of deteriorating wooden sinks. Rachel said, "This is our only washing machine, and as you can see, it has a wringer. So once the clothes have gone through the final rinse, you must flip the switch on the side of the wringer, and place each garment between the two rollers that will squeeze out the water. But be careful. You don't want to catch your fingers in that wringer."

"Oh, I know about wringers. As a little girl, I stood too close to a wringer when my mother was washing clothes. It pulled out a big chunk of my hair."

"Ouch! That must have hurt!" responded Rachel.

"Indeed it did! Another wringer attack happened when I was in high school. I was wringing the excess water from my bathing suit at the YWCA and caught my fingers in the wringer. They weren't broken but badly bruised. So I have been very careful around wringers since." In dismay I looked at the rickety sinks. "Wow! These sinks look well used. The wood seems to be rotting along the sides."

Miss Epps (the author) washing the C Boys' school shirts.

"Yes, they are very old, but fortunately, they still hold water. You'll notice that we have no dryer, so we hang all of the clothes on those lines strung overhead."

I looked up. My eyes followed many lines strung from one end of the room to the other.

"It takes about a day for clothes to dry. And over here are two metal tubs of dry cleaning fluid. Do you have any thing that needs to be dry cleaned?"

"Not today, but I may in the future. It's good to know that we can do this sort of thing by ourselves, when needed."

"It works fairly well. I find that I have to wear rubber gloves, because the temperature of the fluid is miserably cold on your hands. You have to work quickly. Just swish the clothes back and forth a while and wring them out by hand."

"I'll keep that in mind."

"Here is the soap powder on the counter, and I think you'll find the machine is simple to use. Just flip this switch once you've got the powder and the clothes in. I'll leave you to your laundry. I'm going back to the Boys Building."

"I think I can manage by myself now. Thanks, Rachel." As I sorted the laundry, memories of wash day back home flashed through my mind. My mother never trusted the electric washing machine with our good clothing. It was okay for sheets and towels, but for our clothes for school and work, she used a scrub board in a metal tub filled with soapy water. Well, there was no scrub board here, and I was happy to trust this little, white washing machine.

* * *

A few days later, Mr. Echols walked up to me in the dining room after lunch and said, "Miss Epps, I have that painted board ready to place over your radiator . . . any time you want it!"

"Wonderful! Bring it over."

"This afternoon okay?"

"That'll be fine. If I'm not in my room when you knock, I'll be in my sewing room doing some mending. You do know where that is, I suppose?" I smiled, knowing the answer before he gave it.

As expected, he replied with a grin, "I know every square inch of these buildings. I've been here a long time. I'll find you." He found me soon after in my own room with the door wide open. "May I come in?" he asked, holding up the shiny black enameled plank of wood.

"Indeed you can," I said in greeting. "A dressing table at last!"

"Yes, I think this will work nicely for you. Now, if you'll just allow me to put a few nails in the wall to hold the board in place . . . "

"By all means! Do whatever is necessary. I'll be in my sewing room if you need me. I'm going to start on that skirt to hide the radiator right away. By the time you and I are through with this project, it will look like just another piece of furniture."

"That's the idea," he smiled. Mr. Echols was a true handyman of many years experience and was no doubt looking forward to retirement. At times he wore a look of weariness from all of the maintenance work on the three buildings. The board was in place in no time. When I returned with the bolt of material that Ruth Matthews had brought over a few days before, Mr. Echols took one look at the material and said, "Looks like you'll need my hammer and some tacks to attach that cloth to the board."

"Yes, I will."

"I probably don't have enough tacks with me. You keep the hammer, and I'll go get some more tacks," he said, as he turned to leave.

"Thanks." With my yardstick in hand and Mr. Echols out of the way, I took some measurements. The rest of the afternoon was spent cutting material to the right length, and then hemming the skirt edges with the pedal sewing machine. Soon the skirt would hide any evidence of the radiator. The material was fastened half way around the radiator, when I discovered I was just about out of tacks. The first one of my boys home from school stuck his head into the open door.

"Hi, Mis Sepps. Watcha doin'?" It was Floyd. Without waiting for an answer he added, "I got here first. I beat all those other guys! That makes me the fastest runner, huh, Mis Sepps?"

Before I could comment another boy appeared in the doorway. Carl had arrived, "I got here second!"

Willy was right behind him. He too stuck his head in the door and then asked, "We got candy on our beds, Mis Sepps?"

"Go see," I replied. There was an immediate exit of the three boys.

Just as I hammered in another tack, the twins arrived. "Gee! What's that, Miss Epps?" asked Jeff, pointing at the skirt.

"Why are you covering the radiator?" asked Jack.

"Mr. Echols is helping me make a dressing table. What do you think? Does this look nice?"

"Yeah, neat!" they exclaimed together. Then Jack appeared to have second thoughts, "Maybe when it is finished."

About that time Willy burst back into the room. "We got candy on our beds!" he exclaimed to the blonde haired twins.

"Oh boy! Let's go!" yelled one of the twins and off they went.

"Whatcha doin', Mis Sepps?" inquired Willy. Once again I explained my project. I decided to finish this work later, when I would have more tacks and without interruptions from the boys popping in and out of the room.

"You gonna teach me how to iron, Mis Sepps?" I reckoned Willy was just too comfortable with his own unique way of pronouncing my name, that he saw no need to put forth the effort to change. Oh well, I'd save that project for another day. After all, he had just moved up to the C dorm after living with the youngest boys. One adjustment at a time was my thought.

"Why yes, Willy. We can go do that right now. I have two of your good knitted school shirts that need to lose a few wrinkles." Leaving the dressing table skirt project for another day, I slid the hammer underneath the radiator for safe keeping. I got up from my knees and followed the excited Willy to the sewing room.

"This is goin' to be fun!" exclaimed Willy to anyone within hearing distance.

"What is?" asked the approaching Floyd, who didn't want to be left out of anything resembling fun.

"Mis Sepps is gonna teach me how to iron!" responded Willy proudly. The twins were wearing a look of contentment that comes on the faces of kids with their mouths full of candy. They were headed off to the big playroom across the hall. Having had the excitement of learning to iron several years before, they felt no jubilance, other than the fact they were enjoying the candy. They went on their way without comment.

"Awww, ironing's not fun," offered Carl, who had been ironing his own shirts for a whole year.

"Maybe not for you, Carl, but Willy may find it so." I didn't want Carl's comment to dampen Willy's enthusiasm.

Carl's comment stopped Floyd's eager pursuit to "join the fun," even though it appeared Floyd would hang around to judge for himself. In the sewing room I set up the ironing board and plugged in the electric iron as Willy watched with sparkling eyes.

"Since your shirts are cotton knit, I'll set the heat on cotton. Come, Willy, see this word spelled c-o-t-t-o-n on the iron?" Willy walked over to look at the word.

"I don't see nothin'. Where?" I placed my finger by the word, as Willy commented, "Jeez, dat's not a word for first grade. I never seen dat before." Willy appeared agitated. "Dat word is fun-Neeeee."

"Let me see," offered Floyd, ready to accept the challenge. He pushed himself between Willy and me, and then paused, while his eyes searched for the word on the small dial. "That's easy!" He began to slowly pronounce each letter. "C-o-t-t-o-n. Huh, Mis Sepps?"

"Yes, that's right. It spells cotton." I was perhaps getting some insight into the alphabet skills of these two six years olds. *Would Willy be needing some extra help? Time would tell.* "Now Willy, we'll wait a few minutes for the iron to get hot enough to press the wrinkles out of your shirt." I then showed him how to pull the garment onto the ironing board, so that the front of the shirt was ready for pressing, while the back hung below the board. I then handed him the shirt saying, "Okay, now show me that you can do the same with this shirt." Willy took the shirt from my hand.

"Dat's easy. I can do dat." He placed the shirt on the board exactly as I had directed. "See. Eeeee-zy."

I noticed for some time that Willy sprinkled his language gener-ously with "dats," "dems," and "doz." At first I thought he might be of European descent, but Rachel had said, "No, that's just Willy. He hasn't yet conquered the "th" sound. The older kids tease him, and he doesn't like it." That being the case, I would tackle this too at another time.

Once the iron was hot, I demonstrated how to spread the material of the shirt so that the heat from the iron would remove the wrinkles. Then it was Willy's turn. "Gee, just like magic," he exclaimed, very pleased with himself.

"I can do that," said Floyd, edging closer. "Can I be next, Mis Sepps?"

"No! I got *two* shirts," insisted Willy. "You can't be next 'til I'm through." Willy was enjoying being first, and he wasn't about to hurry just to satisfy Floyd.

"Okay, when you're through . . . huh, Mis Sepps?"

"Yes, when Willy is finished, we'll pull out a couple of your school shirts."

Suddenly Carl appeared at the door followed by John Street, "Somebody here to see you, Miss Epps."

"Hey! Miss Epps! I got 'im!" said John.

"You got 'im?" I inquired of John Street, who was standing in the doorway towering over seven year old Carl. "What's Carl done?" I asked a bit puzzled.

"Not Carl . . . the porcupine!"

"You callin' Carl a porcupine?" laughed Floyd in his juvenile attempt to make a joke.

"Shud up, Floyd," demanded the wounded Carl.

Suspecting Floyd's joke was trouble brewing, John hurriedly explained, "No! Carl's not a porcupine! He's my buddy! He found Miss Epps for me. Didn't you, Carl?"

Satisfied that John's quick remarks had canceled Floyd's attempt to bring laughter at Carl's expense, Carl smiled shyly and walked off.

"So you 'got 'im.' When was that?" I asked.

"I saw him gnawing away at the creosote again under the building early last Sunday morning." John quickly glanced around him and then said in a quiet voice, "Tell ya later." Then in his normal voice he acknowl-edged, "Hey! You boys learning to iron?"

"He is. I'm next," offered Floyd. Willy just continued to iron, looking up now and then with a sparkle in his eye, hoping to see John's look of approval.

"Hey! I'm impressed. That's pretty darn good, Willy. Think you could teach me how to do that?"

A big grin crossed Willy's face. "Me just a boy. Me teach a big man how to iron? FunNeee!"

"I don't think that's funny. I need to learn to iron!" said John.

"You get Mis Sepps to teach you. Not me."

"Well, how about you, Floyd? Will you teach me?"

"I don't know how yet. I'm next."

"You mean I have to get in line behind you? That okay, Miss Epps? May I get in line behind Floyd?" he asked with a mischievous grin.

"Tell you what, boys. Let's take a break, and you two boys go off to play, while I talk to John. I'll call you back later."

"Whoopee!" exclaimed Floyd and ran out of the room.

"But I didn't do the arms yet," protested Willy. Looking up at John and then to me, he stated resentfully, "He gettin' in front of me?"

"No, he isn't. I'm not going to teach John how to iron today. That would take too long. I doubt he would learn as quickly as you did, Willy."

John chuckled, "She's right. I'm a slow learner. I'll have to come over some evening after she has put you guys to bed." With a gleam in his eye, John added teasingly, "Why it would probably take her *all* evening to get it through my thick head."

"You slow," pronounced Willy, and then to me said, "Look, I didn't do the arms."

"Oh, that part is easy. I'll show you how to do that when you come back. We'll turn the iron off for now." I turned the dial on the iron to the off position, as Willy reluctantly started to leave the room, looking back over his shoulder.

"I get to finish before Floyd starts," he announced, as he exited the room.

"Of course you will," I assured him.

John followed Willy's exit to the sewing room door and then turned to me, "Mind if I close this door? I don't want the boys to hear."

C Boy pressing school clothes.

"Sure. Go ahead."

With the door closed, John began in a soft voice, "I wanted to tell you out of earshot of the boys, when and how I finally shot the porcupine."

"Okay."

"That morning I waited until everyone had gone to church, and then I got the gun and came to the Boys Building. I knelt in that very same spot, where I showed the porcupine to you the other day. He was still under there. So I took aim and got him in one shot."

I grimaced, "Where is it now?"

"It's in the refrigerator all skinned and ready to be fried. You still game?"

"Yes, I think so." Then I laughed at the thought of me cooking a wild creature. My mother did all of the cooking in our home. *Wouldn't she be surprised at the thought of me doing something in the kitchen, other than warming up food that had already been prepared? Oh, well, how hard could it be? A little grease, a little flour and some salt and pepper . . . I decided I could handle this.* "When are we doing this, John?"

"How about tonight after your boys go to bed? I'll bring everything we need."

"Don't come before eight. I want to make sure that they are all asleep."

"It's a date! See you tonight," and he hurried off.

Is it, now? So now I'm 'dating' one of the maintenance men. Somehow I hadn't thought of this as a 'date,' but that's what he called it. And why not? John's fun! I'll enjoy his company, even if my culinary skills are lacking. Well, at least the nosy B Boys won't observe this 'date' from their windows.

When the dinner bell clanged later on in the early evening, I chanced to enter the arcade at the same time as Dolores. "Know what we're having for dinner?" asked Dolores.

"No."

"Moose steaks. Mrs. Echols told me earlier this afternoon, when I carried the sourdough batter through the kitchen and over to the staff cottage."

"Sourdough batter?"

"Yes, tomorrow is my day off . . . *and* Peggy's. We are going to have sourdough pancakes in the morning over in the staff cottage. And let me tell you . . . *that* will be long after you guys have had breakfast over here in the dining room."

"Planning on sleeping in, huh?"

"You betcha! No getting up at 6:15 a.m. on *my* day off. Luckily Peggy feels the same way, so we leisurely do our own breakfast over there *and* . . . in our pajamas, I might add. Sometimes we even go back to bed after breakfast and don't get up 'til noon," she chuckled.

"No kids to take care of for one whole day. Must be nice."

"Wait 'til you've been here for a while. You'll *love* it."

"I bet I will. Where did the sourdough batter come from? Mrs. Echols prepare that for you?"

"No, Peggy had the batter going before I arrived in Seward. It was growing over in her room, but she decided my room gets more sunshine than hers, so I've had it in my room. I guess heat is an important element in keeping the sourdough going."

By this time, we had arrived at our respective tables, and one of the C Girls began to complain to Dolores, "Miss Morey, look! We're havin' moose and I can't cut it," she said in disgust. "Will you cut it up for me?"

"Me too," popped in Van, the youngest boy at her table. "I can't cut mine."

"Yes, yes. I'll help you both and anybody else who needs help." And to me she added in a quiet voice, "You're lucky that you don't have any real little ones at your table. This always happens on moose day. I spend so much time cutting *their* meat; I hardly have time to eat my own."

Trying to get a piece of moose chewed enough to swallow, I asked, "Why is the meat so tough?"

"Mrs. Echols says that's because we only get moose that has been killed by accident. It hasn't been skinned or bled right. That's why it tastes "gamy."

"How does a hunter kill a moose by accident?"

"The train hits them. We get most of our moose from the Alaska Railroad. The moose wander onto the tracks, and even though the engineer blows the whistle, often the snow is so high on both sides of the tracks, they can't get out of the way. So since the moose can't outrun the train, they get hit. It's already tired meat even before the train kills the moose. Mrs. Echols says that makes a *big* difference."

Pammy, one of the B Girls, spoke up, "Miss Morey, they didn't put any ketchup on our table. Shall I go to the kitchen and get a bottle?"

"Oh heavens, yes!" replied Dolores. "We can't eat moose without ketchup." And to me she added, "It helps to kill some of the wild taste." Immediately, I remembered my very first meal at Jesse Lee Home and the awful moose soup. I was *not* looking forward to this meal. I noticed when the meal began; nobody ate before several generous dollops of ketchup smothered the moose steak. I did the same. Much to my surprise, the ketchup made the meat edible, and I was grateful to Mrs. Echols for having added ketchup to the menu.

Dolores never bothered to sit. She just went to both sides of the table with her table knife trying to cut the tough steak into bite size pieces for those who wanted help. And to me she said, "My friend Kyle says that when moose is properly handled after the kill and cooked with care by a creative cook, it can taste very much like beef. That's never been our experience here with the moose we get." To the children she added, "Chew that moose well. You need to do that for proper digestion." Then Dolores finally sat down to attack her own piece of meat.

"I'm chewing mine like chewing gum," said Pammy. "I just chew and chew and chew. And it's still tough!"

In disgust Van said, "I'm tired of chewin'. I'm gonna spit it out," and the chunk of moose fell from his mouth onto his plate.

"Oooooooo, look what Van did, Miss Morey!" said Pammy, wearing a look of disgust.

"No, Van. You must swallow your meat. Otherwise, it won't do your body any good. *Don't* spit it out," commanded Dolores. Van picked up the chewed meat with his fingers and put it back in his mouth.

"Oooooo, he is so gross! I don't like sitting across from Van. Can I change seats, Miss Morey?" Van continued to chew, seemingly oblivious to Pammy's complaint.

"Now swallow it, Van," instructed Dolores. "And no, Pammy, you may not change seats. And it's 'may I,' not 'can I.' Keep in mind Van is only five years old. By the time he is your age, I venture to say that his table manners will be as good as yours." Pammy rolled her eyes in doubt.

"I did it, Miss Morey," gulped Van.

"Good boy!" said Dolores. "See what I mean, Betty Jane?" looking to her left towards me.

"Indeed I do." I glanced around my own table but saw no display of bad manners. Also it seemed the children were too busy chewing to engage in much chatter. My mind began to ponder if that wild meat taste was in store for me tonight with the porcupine. Oh, well, I was already committed to the porcupine fry. Hopefully, John would remember to bring a bottle of ketchup.

That night, after the bedtime story, I went to each bed tucking the boys in with a kiss on the forehead and said good night. The giggling I heard in the room was always coming from Carl's bed. Once again Carl was hiding under the covers, and refused to present his head for any show of affection. His bed was always the last I visited, since it was close to the doorway leading out of the dorm. For some reason, this act was embarrassing for seven year old Carl, and although he may have wanted the kiss, something in his make-up would not allow him to receive it.

I kept hoping eventually that he would be accepting of my affection, but his ducking under the covers told me to honor his body language. And I did. It seemed enough for Carl that I tried.

By 8:00 o'clock I was waiting for John in the sewing room with the door open. I hadn't read more than a page or two of my book before he appeared loaded down with a hot plate, the porcupine, a skillet, and ingredients to carry forth this anticipated project. "My goodness, John, I do believe you have tried to bring everything we need in one trip."

"It's my Texas camping experience. Learned how to accomplish such as a star Boy Scout."

"I'm impressed."

"That's the whole idea," he grinned. "Where do you want this stuff?"

I had cleaned off a section of the wide counter against the wall. "There is an electrical outlet near this counter, where we can plug in the hot plate; so just unload your stuff here, and that should give us plenty of room to work."

"Fine," said John in a big masculine voice that prompted me to close the sewing room door.

"We should try to keep our voices down. I think they are all asleep, but you never know."

"Right," replied John, dropping his voice to a whisper.

"Well, we don't have to whisper, but we can try to converse softly."

"Gotcha." John began to identify items, as he placed each on the counter, as if to let me know why he had brought each of them. The skillet had a lid on it, and when I removed the lid, I saw a clump of shortening waiting to carry out its role in the porcupine feast. "Oh, yeah," continued John, "and the shortening is ready to be heated." From another box, he carefully removed a cup filled with flour, a salt and pepper set that he no doubt had removed from one of the dining room tables, two plates, and some silverware. "Think this will do it?" he asked, quite pleased with himself.

"John, I don't think you have forgotten a thing. Hmmm, it would be easier to flour the porcupine pieces if we had a paper bag to shake them in." I had seen my mother do that with chicken for many a Sunday dinner, although I had never done it. My mother was a fastidious person, who would rather do all the cooking herself, than have her kids in the kitchen making a mess. Now I had to devise a different plan.

"Want me to go back to the kitchen and look?" asked John. "Although . . . I've never seen a simple paper bag there except those little ones used for Sunday picnic suppers. But I don't know where they are. Most of our food comes in large boxes . . . not bags."

"No, never mind. We'll just pour the cup of flour out on one of the plates and roll the porcupine pieces around in the flour. By the way, I'm glad you carved the porcupine into individual pieces before you brought it over. Why don't you plug in the hot plate?"

"Yeah, I cut the creature up over in the kitchen, while I was waiting for eight o'clock to come around. Hope I brought enough flour. I've never done this, you know." He plugged in the heating unit.

"We'll make it do. Since this fellow has lost his quills and fur, there isn't all that much to him, is there?" I carefully placed the porcupine pieces onto the other plate.

"No, I was kinda surprised myself." The shortening began to melt and sizzle almost immediately. The sound brought attention to the skillet. I walked to the heating unit and checked the setting.

"John, I'm going to turn it down to medium. Otherwise, it will brown too fast on the outside before it is done on the inside."

"See, I knew I needed help with this. Otherwise, I'd probably end up with charred porcupine pieces with raw meat on the inside."

I laughed. "Well, it's sort of the blind leading the blind on this one, since neither of us have fried porcupine before." Well, I had never fried *anything* before, but John didn't need to know that. I began to roll the individual pieces into the flour and then place each one into the hot fat. Fortunately they all fit into the skillet.

"Hey! It's beginning to smell like chicken frying. Maybe we're doing something right," exclaimed John.

"Here, John, take this fork and turn the pieces over as they brown, and I'll take our two plates to the bathroom sink to wash the flour and porcupine drippings off."

"Will do," he dutifully remarked and with fork in hand stood over the sizzling meat ready to do as told. I left the room and returned shortly with the two cleaned plates.

"Now all we have to do is wait for the cooking to be over," I said, observing John still at his post as porcupine chef.

"Shouldn't we put some salt and pepper on it at some point?" asked John.

"Yes, let's do that before you turn each piece over." I moved the salt and pepper shakers closer to John.

"So far, so good," said John. "We haven't awakened any of the C Boys yet."

"I think not," I agreed. "I'll just step out into the little hallway and see if I hear anything." I opened the door quietly and walked the few steps to the doorway of the dorm. Sure enough all was quiet. On my return I commented, "I believe this is going to work, John. All I heard were a few gentle snores."

"I don't see how they can be sound asleep so early. I never went to bed at seven when I was their age," commented John.

"Nor I, but I guess in institutional living there is no choice. And you know the light in the summer nights doesn't seem to bother them much at all. I pull those shabby shades down to block out as much light as possible from those tall, vertical windows, but light still creeps in around the sides."

"Well, most of them were born and raised in Alaska, and I guess they've learned to expect this seasonal act of nature this far north."

"You know, John . . . tell me what you think. My observation is that more is expected of these children than from the average home in most communities. Certainly more so than when I was growing up, and these kids come through for you."

"They simply have no choice. It's institutional living."

"And everybody has to do their share," I nodded in agreement. "They work hard, and they play hard. I guess that helps them sleep." I walked over to the frying meat. "Here, let me do this for a while. It's my turn. You just sit in that chair and relax. After all, you did most of the work before you arrived over here tonight."

He handed me the fork. "Don't mind if I do." John settled into one of the two chairs in the room and rested his arm on the small sewing table. Tell me about you, Betty Jane. Hear you just graduated from the University of Tennessee."

"That I did," I sighed. "Glad that's over. And you, John? I hear you have to go back to school this fall. So guess you haven't graduated yet."

"Nope. Got one more year. Then it will be a Baptist seminary somewhere."

"Oh? You're going into the ministry. Well, you *do* have some years ahead of you. How did you happen to come to Jesse Lee Home?"

"I knew the Matthews back in Texas. I corresponded with Elwin, and he offered me this job for the summer. But hey! We're supposed to be talking about you. You tricked me. Now let's talk about you."

"Well, what do you want to know? You know that like Peggy and Phyllis, I'm a U.S.-2, but we're expected to stay for three years instead of two."

"Why *is* that?"

"I guess it's because it costs the Mission Board more money to send short-term missionaries out to the U.S. territories, than within the continental states. In fact, we were told in training if we decided to shorten our commitment from the three years, we would have to return some of the money it costs the Board to send us so far."

"That true for Hawaii and Puerto Rico too? Does the Mission Board send anyone to those places?"

"Not Puerto Rico this year, but two people went to Hawaii. And yes, that applies to Hawaii too."

"Lucky, huh? Can't imagine anyone wanting to come home early from there."

"I've thought of going to Hawaii after my stint here at Jesse Lee Home. I assume they have similar needs there. I'd have to ask specifically for that state."

"One would think institutions for children are in every state or territory, as the case may be. Saaaay, how's the porcupine coming? Done yet?"

"All the pieces are brown," I observed carefully lifting each piece with the fork to check the color of the meat. "I'll turn the heat down low, and we'll let it cook a little while longer, just to make sure it all gets cooked all the way through. It does smell good, doesn't it?"

"Yes, it's making me hungry."

"It won't be long now." We continued the conversation speaking of our lives back home for about fifteen minutes. "I believe we can eat it now, John. Shall we give it a try?"

"I'm ready, willing, and waiting."

"Here's your plate. Why don't you come over and pick out a piece you want?" John left his chair and accepted the fork offered him. He chose a hearty piece of meat to accommodate his growing appetite, while I chose a smaller piece, not sure how my taste buds would receive this meat from the wild. Sitting at the small table, we began to bite into pieces and chew in quiet. Our eyes met. John seemed to be enjoying the meat, but I found it a bit tough. Since this critter wasn't running in front of a train when John shot him, I wondered *why* it was so tough. *We cooked it just like chicken, and chicken was always tender and tasty.*

"What do you think, Betty Jane? We did pretty good, huh?"

"Well, my piece is a bit tough. I don't know about yours."

"Yeah, a little but it's good. How do you find the taste?"

"Not quite the taste of chicken is it?"

"It has a little bit of that wild flavor but I *like* it." said John firmly.

"I bet you even like the moose taste then."

"I'm getting used to it, but I'd prefer a big, juicy Texas beef steak any day." A few pieces later, we decided that we had had enough of the porcupine. "I'll take the rest over and put it in the refrigerator. If you want more, you'll know where it is," offered John.

"I think this will do me, John. I can now say that I have had the porcupine experience. We probably could have improved the flavor if we had thought to add onions, garlic or some seasoning to diffuse the wild taste. Even a bottle of ketchup might have helped."

"True, the wild taste takes some getting used to. I'll carry all this stuff back to the kitchen and clean the skillet, plates and silverware."

"I'm sorry I can't leave the dorm to help you, John, but I'm on duty tonight, as you know. Here, I'll help you put all of this back in the boxes."

"No problem," said John. "I can handle this. I just need to clean up well, so Mrs. Echols will let me use her kitchen again sometime."

"If you are going out to shoot something else, better hurry. You don't have many days left do you?"

"No, and speaking of that, would you go out with me on one of your nights off before I go? There's some pretty places around here I'd like to show you. Like nothing you've ever seen in Tennessee! The scenery here is out of this world. I can borrow the Jesse Lee Home truck."

"Sure, John, let's do that." I had decided that John was a very nice young man and I liked him. "And thank you for sharing the porcupine with me. Eating porcupine for the very first time is something! This will be a first that I can write home about."

"Just give me a chance, Betty Jane, and I'll give you even more to write home about," he said flirtatiously with a sparkle in his big brown eyes.

I bet you would, I thought, but I wasn't going to say that aloud to this young man, who was about to exit my life, almost as quickly as he entered. I wondered if John had "dated" any of the other single house-mothers. And I knew just the person to ask. Dolores would know. I made a mental note to ask her. And thus ended the first "date" with John.

* * *

The next morning, when the wake-up bell did its usual loud clanging at 6:15 a.m., Dolores and Peggy never heard it. Peggy was up first at 8:30 trying to be as quiet as she could in the staff cottage kitchen, as she prepared for their weekly sourdough pancake breakfast. She needed only add the milk and flour, as the sourdough had its own rising agent. At the right room temperature, she and Dolores had managed to keep the sourdough starter growing for months on end. It was true that the slight sour taste of the dough was not appetizing to some, but this was definitely a touch of Alaska that these two relished. Many of the early gold miners had carried sourdough starters and passed it from one gold miner to the next during the great Alaskan gold rush many years ago. Always a small amount was left to grow in a container and carried throughout the Klondike, as the men and women searched for gold in the early 1900's. Like Peggy, they needed only to add liquid and flour and leave a little in the container to continue growing with the bread rising agent. These adventurous souls soon became known as 'sourdoughs.' That term is still used to this day to describe any long term Alaskan. Newcomers are referred to as 'cheechakos' but that's another story.

The staff cottage was located a few hundred feet behind the middle building of Jesse Lee Home, where the dining room and kitchen were housed. It had actually been a chicken house many years ago, when the staff tried to keep a few farm animals and chickens. This small cottage actually had four rooms and a bath. There were two bedrooms, a living room with a dining table at one end, and a kitchen. It was a welcome respite away from the children, that every house parent needed to regenerate energies for another week. It was nice to be away from the challenge of settling juvenile disputes and the stress of feeling fully responsible for a large family of ten to eleven children. Working at Jesse Lee Home was no nine to five job by any means. One night off and one whole day off each week was looked upon almost as a luxury by the staff.

Peggy would allow Dolores as much time to sleep-in as she desired. But Dolores awoke and looked at the clock at a quarter to nine. She had gotten over two extra hours of sleep, and she felt wonnnnderful! She heard Peggy in the kitchen and sprang from her bed to allow this special day to begin. "Oh, no you don't, Peggy. You're not doing all the work for breakfast."

"Good morning, Dolores! I see you are up. I hope I didn't wake you. I tried to be quiet, but the walls are thin in this chicken house."

"It was time to get up, but do let me help."

"I have a surprise for us," announced Peggy with a note of glee in her voice. "Mrs. Echols let me have a few pieces of bacon to enjoy with our pancakes. I'll start frying the bacon, while you go ahead and wash up. By then the griddle will be ready for the pancakes. You can do the honors there."

"It's a deal," responded Dolores, and she went into the bathroom to freshen up.

At breakfast the two exchanged stories of the antics of their charges during the past week. Now it was time to laugh at what had seemed irritations, when confronted with an erring child.

"Let me tell you what Boris did!" announced Dolores.

"The twins' brother?" asked Peggy.

"Yes. You know I pride myself on keeping a close check on the boys before they board the bus for church. On Sundays they look downright angelic all cleaned up with shoes polished and wearing white shirts and ties."

"Yes, I've noticed that too. My A Girls have that special look when dressed in their finest."

"Last Sunday when we got home from church, I was standing outside in the hall of the B Boys' dorm, when I heard all of this laughter. Curiously, I walked in and saw all the boys gathered around Boris just laughing their heads off. I asked what was so funny. Horace stopped laughing long enough to say, 'Lookee there, Miss Morey! Boris went to church in his pajamas!' "

"Yeah," added Clyde, "He just pulled his pants and jacket on over his p.j.'s."

"His pajamas?" asked Peggy in surprise.

"Yes!" nodded Dolores, "And one of them said, 'And he's done it before!' "

"Tell me, why on earth why?" asked Peggy.

"You tell me," replied Dolores, shaking her head. "Boris just sat there red faced, not knowing if he should laugh or cry."

"Someone squealed on him, huh?"

"Obviously, Boris had annoyed someone, and this was payback time. Looks like I'm going to have to tighten up the screws again. No more complacency!" They both laughed.

"You take the prize this week, Dolores. I can't top that."

* * *

That evening Phyllis knocked on my door, "You ready, Betty Jane?"

"I think so. Come on in." Phyllis walked into the room and found me standing before the round mirror over the radiator dressing table with its unfinished skirt hanging awry. "Will this do? You said to wear a full skirt if I had one."

"Yes, *your* skirt is fine, but what's happening with that skirt going around your radiator?"

"Oh, that!" I responded looking down at my unfinished interior decorating. "I had to stop because I ran out of tacks. Mr. Echols was going to bring me more, but he must have gotten involved with something else. I'll have to remind him tomorrow. What do most of the people wear that go to the Square Dance Club?" I asked.

"Some of them wear traditional square dancing outfits. They must order them out of a catalog. I've never seen such in stores in Seward. And some just wear their regular clothes. That full skirt will work nicely."

"Well, you certainly look like you are ready for square dancing. That's very nice," I remarked, as I took in Phyllis attractively dressed in a full cotton printed skirt and peasant blouse.

"Sorry, we don't have any transportation but our feet. It's only a short walk below Jesse Lee Home."

"Where are the square dances held?"

"The army uses Seward as a place for rest and relaxation. So they built a recreation center just below us here. It has a large room with an added kitchen and is big enough for parties. The Square Dance Club brings the records for music, and often we have a caller. It's fun. You'll like it!"

"I'm sure I will. Shall we go?" As soon as we ended the short walk to the 'Rec Center' and entered the door, it was apparent that Phyllis was popular. She was a happy, attractive young woman with a ready laugh and a delightful sense of humor. She was two or three years older than I and was surprisingly sensitive about her age. That puzzled me. Phyllis had come from Boston and had only learned of the U.S.-2 program several years after her college graduation. She had been out into the working world for a few years but was still young enough to enter this short-term mission program. She realized most of her fellow U.S.-2's were younger, a fact that bothered no one but Phyllis.

"Now, just listen to the callers and they tell us exactly what moves to make. The guys will push you through if you are not sure. Don't worry about making a mistake."

There was no lack of partners. The Seward Square Dance Club attracted lots of bachelors from the long shoring and fishing industries. They came in all shapes and sizes and all manner of personalities. Their education background varied from high school drop-outs to well educated, professional, young men. However, when they opened their mouths, it was easy to tell one from the other. The three Methodist institutions provided young nurses from the hospital, house mothers from the Jesse Lee Home, and single staff from the Tuberculosis Sanatorium. Married couples of all ages were active in the club as well. In fact, this club was one of the most popular social opportunities available the year around. Since no drinking was allowed on the premises, any young, single woman felt safe in attending. There were never any ugly scenes of alcoholic behavior, as one might find in an Alaskan bar. If inebriated persons did arrive, they soon got the message that this was not a place where they were welcome. The men in the Club quietly saw to that.

Phyllis proved to be an excellent square dancer. She knew all of the calls and all of the steps and often helped the guys who had trouble interpreting the callers' directions. Some of the dances were simple, which made it fun for newcomers. Others could be rather intricate, and a guy needed to stay focused to lead his partner. Being new, I relied heavily on partners pushing me through the patterns until I became familiar with the calls.

At the end of the evening, when we were walking back, I said to Phyllis, "Thanks, Phyl. That was fun! What a change from living and working with kids twenty-four hours a day! We needed that!"

"Now you see why I wanted them to assign your night off on Thursdays. Besides it just being fun, it gives us the opportunity to meet adults of all ages from town. On Sunday we don't really get to socialize with many of the adults at church. The bus departs so soon after the church service."

"Well, *you* seemed to know that whole room full of people tonight, *and* you tried to see that I met them all. I'll never remember all of their names."

"I bet you'll remember Big Ed!" Phyllis laughed. "What did you think of dancing with him?"

"Wow! He is something else! I was never so surprised, as when he literally picked me up off of the floor and swung me around in the air. He must be the biggest guy in town!"

"Yeah, he's all muscle. He probably has zero fat. Dancing with Big Ed is like a ride at the State Fair. Some of the women love it, but some shy away from him."

"He must be fun on a date. Is he?"

"No. Believe it or not this great big Scandinavian is painfully shy. It's like pulling teeth to engage him in conversation. He's a longshoreman and I couldn't even get him talking about that. But he *loves* to dance."

"Well, that was obvious. Fortunately, square dancing doesn't allow time to engage in much more than polite phrases. I didn't even notice his shyness."

"Did you dance with the coach? Now *there's* an opposite."

"Oh, the little short fellow? Not much taller than me?"

"That's the one. They say he throws tantrums at the basketball games. Some say he puts on more of a show than the game itself."

"He's the high school basketball coach?"

"Yes . . . and the whole town attends the basketball games. The coach's ranting and raving is very well known and quite the attraction."

"He seemed pleasant enough but like I said, you don't get much of a conversation going in a square dance. Everybody is focusing on what to do next."

"No, that part of him only comes out at the games. I've never seen one. Basketball doesn't interest me."

"What does interest you in Seward, now that you've lived here for a couple of years?"

"I'll show you tomorrow on our day off. We can take a picnic lunch and walk into town. If a ship is docked, music will be blasting at its arrival, and I know some of the staff aboard some of the ships. That gives me the opportunity to visit a ship now and then. If not, I'll show you a waterfall that drops right into Resurrection Bay. And then I'll show you some other neat places in town."

"Great. Are we sleeping in the staff cottage tonight?"

"You bet! Just grab your p.j.'s, a change of clothing for tomorrow, and don't worry about breakfast. There's dry cereal there and milk in the refrigerator. A toaster is always there too and a coffee pot. We won't starve. When we get to town, we can even buy a hamburger if you like. I'll show you the grocery store down there and some neat little restaurants."

"Now that sounds like a great day off. I'll meet you in the cottage later." And then we went our separate ways to gather what was needed for a day away from the demands of our young charges.

Chapter 11

A FIRST DAY OFF WITH PHYL AND BOYS PLAY 'KING OF THE HILL' ON DIRTY SHEETS

At 8:00 o'clock the next morning, I opened my eyes and looked around the room. It was so quiet. Where was I? Ah yes . . . the staff cottage. I glanced at the other bed and saw that Phyllis was still sleeping. I hadn't been awakened by the loud clanging wake-up bell. I was looking forward to this Friday. I got up quietly without waking Phyllis and checked out the food in the kitchen. Yes, there was dry cereal on the shelf beside the gas stove, and just as Phyllis had mentioned, there was indeed milk inside the refrigerator.

Taking the first turn in the small bathroom, I was soon washed and ready to get out of my pajamas and into my clothes for the day. I tiptoed back into the bedroom.

"You had breakfast?" asked Phyllis lazily.

"No, thought I'd wait for you, but I *am* through in the bathroom, if you want in there."

"Pushy, pushy, pushy . . . and on my day off."

I chuckled. "I'm sorry. Guess I'm just too eager to start this day of freedom that you spoke of so glowingly."

Phyllis threw off the covers and placed her feet on the floor. "Oh, it's *time* to get up. We don't want to sleep through all of this day." She shuffled out of the room and headed to the bathroom saying, "Go ahead and start eating. This won't take long."

"I'll get dressed first," I responded getting out of my sleepwear. I then slipped into clean underwear and flannel lined blue jeans. The pants would keep my legs warm, if we found ourselves down by the water with the wind blowing off of Resurrection Bay. Long sleeved shirts were definitely a must for this southern girl, who was now experiencing temperatures in the low 60's instead of the high 80's. My navy blue jacket with the red wool lining would work well for the walk into town . . . if needed. With the bed made and clothes put away, I went into the kitchen. I was enjoying a bowl of Wheaties, when Phyllis joined me all dressed and ready for the day.

"How are the Wheaties? Don't know how long they have been here. They may be stale," she commented.

"They're fine," I replied with a mouth full.

"What? No coffee? Didn't you find it?"

"I'm not much of a coffee drinker." That was only a half truth. I had never made a cup of coffee in my life. I simply didn't know how. "You go ahead and make coffee, if you want it."

"Oh no, in that case, I'll make a cup of tea. Want some?" asked Phyllis.

"You're talking *hot* tea, aren't you?"

"Yes, I am. Let's see what's here." Phyllis began to read the names on the limited variety of teas stored on one of the shelves. "Not much of a selection, I have to admit."

"Never mind, I'll pass on that too. You're talking to a southern girl, who has *never* had tea any way but iced."

"Iced tea," mused Phyllis. "Don't think Mrs. Echols has *ever* had that on the menu. In fact, in the dining room, it's coffee or powdered milk most of the time."

"So I noticed."

"We'll just have to teach you how to enjoy *hot* tea, if you are to survive around here."

"Okay, but not today. I'm still trying to learn to appreciate powdered milk. The sugar on the cereal helps."

"Believe it or not, you *can* get used to it. Notice I didn't say you can learn to *enjoy* it or even *appreciate* it . . . just get used to it." Phyllis turned on the gas on the stove to heat the water for tea. She had chosen a teabag from a large box labeled Liptons. "One of these days we'll let you make some iced tea, and we'll sit around all afternoon sipping. Or would you rather have a mint julep? That's what they drink in the South, isn't it? Doubt we'd have any fresh lemon for it though. Is that a must?"

"Absolutely for iced tea. Don't know about the julep. That sounds more like the cotton plantation beverages over in west Tennessee. East Tennessee is mountain folk. Ever hear of the Great Smoky Mountains?"

"Yes, I think those mountains drifted into a geography lesson or two in our Boston schools. And you're from east Tennessee . . . Knoxville is it?"

"Yes, it's called the Gateway to the Great Smoky Mountains."

"Are they as great as these around here?"

"Well, they are different. For one thing they have trees on top of them."

"The lack of trees mean these are higher. You can see where the tree line stops on all of the mountains around here."

"I haven't seen any roads winding up to these mountain tops. You can drive right up to the top of the Smoky Mountains."

"You're right. You gotta use your feet to get to the top of Alaska's mountains. But not me, I'd rather use my feet for square dancing."

"So I noticed, and you do it very well. That really was fun last night, Phyl."

"Good. I was hoping you'd like it. It keeps me sane, especially during the winter months." The boiling water whistled in the tea kettle. "Oops! Looks like my tea water is ready!"

"That Boston Tea Party thing drifted down to the Knoxville schools. No wonder *you* are a tea drinker."

Phyllis poured the boiling water over the teabag in her cup. "Actually, it's a very comforting hot beverage when you live in the north. Perhaps you'll eventually find relaxing with a hot cup of tea takes the edge off of daily frustrations."

"Maybe . . . but right now that sounds no more appealing than you offering me hot ice cream. No, don't think Southerners were meant to drink their tea hot, but I'll give it a try." Phyllis got up to get another teabag and cup. But I protested, "No, no! Not today! I'll have to work myself up to that one!"

Phyllis sat down saying, "All right then, whenever you are ready."

In short time we were walking on the rocky road leading into town. I noticed a prickly plant growing along the road as high as my shoulders. "What is that plant?" I asked curiously.

"Beware of that one. That's devil's club! It's a mean one. Try not to touch it. If you get one of its thorns in your skin, you have to just leave it there, until your body takes care of it. The skin around it gets very sore, and it takes a while to have the discomfort go away."

"Why is that?"

Phyllis began to laugh, "I don't know, Betty Jane. I'm not a botanist. I'm just telling you what they told me when I arrived. I guess it's because the thorn sticks under your skin like a fishhook."

"Hmmm," I mused, eyeing the dreaded plant curiously, "I'll try to stay clear of these wicked fellows then."

Some time later we had reached the small business district of Seward, and Phyl gave me a running commentary on where I could find what. The grocery store was very small in comparison to the stores back home. I suspected prices were higher too, but neither of us was interested in pursuing that project on this quick walking tour of the town.

"The best souvenirs are here in the Alaska Shop. All the tourists come in here from the cruise ships. The local florist operates in the back." Once inside the building, I browsed the Alaskan jewelry with its artistic arrangements of gold nuggets, ivory, and jade. My eyes were focused on the tiny price tags on the individual boxes in the glass case, when Phyllis came up behind me saying, "Ready to go? Believe it or not, there is more to see in this tiny metropolis called Seward. And I must show you a good place to eat. It's called The Bakery."

"Good. I was just checking out the prices on the jewelry."

"Did you want to buy some?"

"Not now, but maybe later for Christmas presents." I followed Phyllis out the door, and we headed down toward Resurrection Bay.

"Yes, I sent some of that Alaskan jewelry home for presents, but I found the plain ivory wasn't appreciated, as much as anything with a gold nugget on it. Folks back home don't realize how much the walrus ivory costs up here. On a U.S.-2's salary, I can't afford to buy much."

"No, I can't imagine $125.00 a month goes very far." We had reached the end of the main street that stopped right at the railroad tracks.

Phyllis looked to her right, "Oh, look! One of the Alaska Steamships is docked. Got your camera ready? This is a great spot to take pictures with the ship and the blue waters of the Bay in the background."

"I agree!" I removed the leather cover from the slide camera the Knoxville District Woman's Society had given to me. I knew they expected pictures of this mission experience, and this would be my first effort to begin that on-going project.

We walked to where the ship was tied up at the dock. "Ummm, don't think I know anyone working on *this* ship," remarked Phyllis, as she looked up at the few crew members in view on the decks. "But it will do for a background for photos. Here, B.J., you sit here on the edge of the dock, and I'll get a shot of you and the ship. Then you can take me."

Suddenly I realized that in less than a day, Phyliss and I had felt so comfortable with each other, a shorter version of our names had just naturally fallen into the conversation. I had called her "Phyl" at breakfast, and now Phyllis was calling me "B.J." It felt good. It felt right. Perhaps this was the beginning of a lasting friendship.

The surrounding mountains with patches of last season's snow clinging to the tops gave the finishing touch to each camera scene. Once the picture taking was completed, Phyl continued as my personal tour guide. "Let's walk on down the road here along the Bay. I want to show you this water-fall." Very soon our ears were filled with the roaring sound of an enormous amount of water falling. A short walk away from the business district, we came upon a large volume of water escaping from the land above on our right. Water was cascading about thirty feet down a small cliff right beside the road and no more than four feet from the occasional moving traffic. "Whatta ya think of that, B.J.?" Phyl shouted, as we approached.

"Wow! Where is it coming from?" I yelled.

"Not sure. Some lake . . . I guess," said Phyl raising her voice even louder.

"It's so close! I like it, but I'm getting wet! How about you?"

Phyllis jumped out of the way of the spray from the falls. "We can go back now. Just wanted you to see it!" she shouted. Our voice levels returned to normal, as we walked away from the water.

"Do you bowl?" asked Phyllis.

"I have but I'm not the greatest."

"I'll show you our lone bowling alley. It's down the road here in the other direction, a block from the main drag. It's just something to do that is different on one's day off."

Inside the bowling alley, I looked around at the sparse group actively bowling. "Not many people here," I remarked.

"Well, it's the middle of the day. There are probably more here in the evening. Wanna play sometime?"

"Sure, but right now, where is that little restaurant you spoke of? All this walking has made me hungry. Maybe after lunch we can bowl a game or two."

"You're right. Let's go to The Bakery and get some goodies." We returned to the main street and walked a couple of blocks north, turned the corner on our left, and there was The Bakery, only a few steps away.

"Ohhh, those aromas! I love it!" I remarked, as we opened the door to this small establishment. The glass case held pastries of all kinds. We viewed a large variety of cookies, bear claws, doughnuts, cream puffs, muffins, and many other baked goods. Further down the counter was a supply of fresh sandwiches and soft drinks. "Shall we select dessert first?" I asked.

"By all means," replied Phyllis. "Mrs. Echols never puts any of these fancy morsels on the table. What will it be?"

"Decisions, decisions," I responded. Finally we selected a couple of fancy pastries each and then decided we would split a sandwich.

"I like roast beef. It would be a nice change from all of that moose we get at Jesse Lee," suggested Phyl.

"I see your point, but I would much prefer the ham. Shall we each buy our own?"

"Nahhh, I'll split the ham with you. Once we have eaten these rich desserts, we'll only have room for a half sandwich."

"Okay, then. How about a couple of cokes? We never get pop at Jesse Lee," I suggested.

"You go ahead, B.J., I think I want a cup of coffee."

"What? No hot tea?"

"Not this time. The aroma of that fresh coffee brewing has me hooked."

We paid for the meals and sat at a table by a window, eating and watching the people go by. After a while I remarked, "Folks sure don't dress up much here to go to town, do they?"

"Oh, so you've noticed the absence of high fashion here in Seward, huh?" chuckled Phyllis. "Notice all of the Alaska tuxedos? Poor dears. They actually think they *are* all dressed up. Now doesn't that sound like a remark from a proper Bostonian?"

"Proper, huh? Guess I'd better watch my wardrobe around you."

"Just kidding, B.J. I couldn't care less what the men in this town wear. Actually, I find Alaska a welcome respite from the demands of Boston aristocracy, not that my family was a part of Boston's high society. Still that kind of stuff sifts down into us lower classes and makes us think it is of some importance. Obviously, it isn't to Sewardites."

Just how would you describe the "Alaskan Tuxedo?" I want to make sure I am observing what you are.

Looking out the window, Phyllis declared, "There! The guy crossing the street! He's wearing one. See? The pants and top are made of a heavy corded material, probably similar to gabardine. The jacket is more like a loose fitting shirt hanging below the waist, and instead of buttons, it has snaps. I suppose these suits are comfortable, and mostly, you see those string ties being worn with them instead of regular ties."

"Well, you won't catch me telling these men folk they are out of step with high fashion. From the number of them wearing those suits, it appears their favorite color is called 'drab.' "

"That's about the only color they come in," laughed Phyllis. "Now wait a minute. I take that back. I believe that I have seen two shades of drab. One is a definite grayish drab . . ." She was interrupted by the door opening. A little bell rang to let the clerk know another customer had arrived.

"You mean like the one walking into the bakery right now?" I asked ever so quietly.

"No, that's the other color," responded Phyllis, lowering her voice. "If you look more closely, you'll notice it has a greenish tinge to it."

I tried to observe this "Alaskan Tuxedo" without allowing the stranger to recognize that I was indeed staring at him. "Hmm, I see what you mean," I observed.

Suddenly the stranger glanced in our direction and called to Phyllis, "Hi, there, Phyl! Good to see you. Got the day off?"

"At last!" she replied. He walked straight to our table.

"Hello, Kevin, this is Betty Jane. She is one of our new housemothers. Kevin is from the Square Dance Club."

"I'm happy to meet you," I responded.

"Why yes, I saw you at the square dance. Did you enjoy our club?"

"Yes, very much. It was fun. I'm not a very good dancer yet, but maybe it will come."

"It will. When Nona and I first started, we felt the same way, but now we can keep up with the best of them. Can't we, Phyl?"

"That you can! How is Nona?"

"I just put her on the plane to visit our daughter Outside. She'll be gone a couple of weeks."

"A bachelor for two weeks. Can you handle that, Kevin?" asked Phyl.

"I dunno. You wanna come down and fix supper for me some night? Take pity on a poor, starving bachelor?"

"I'm afraid you wouldn't fare well from my cooking. I don't cook."

"Then come down and I'll cook *you* a meal. Actually, I'm a pretty good cook."

"Hmm, that so? Well, maybe I'll let you prove that pronouncement sometime. Although I'm beginning to have my doubts. You realize that you are in here to buy a meal the very minute your wife leaves town."

"Just getting some doughnuts for the office staff. They work better when I treat 'em."

Phyliss explained to me saying, " Kevin works for ACS that handles all of Alaska's long distance calls."

"Interesting," I answered.

"Got a new man that just joined the staff," said Kevin. " Wants to come to the square dances. Wantcha to meet him."

"Then bring him with you next Thursday," offered Phyllis.

"I just might do that. I better get those doughnuts. The office knows I'm here to get them. They'll be wondering where I am."

"Gotta keep'em happy," agreed Phyl.

"Nice to meet you, Betty Jane."

"Thank you. Same here." Kevin walked to the counter. We put on our jackets and left the bakery.

When we returned to the bowling alley, I searched diligently for a light-weight ball. "I just can't handle these heavy bowling balls. Don't they have any lighter ones?"

"Let's ask the guy." We walked up to the young man behind the counter and asked.

"No, ma'am. Most of the women special order the lighter balls. We can order you one if you'd like." We looked at each other with concern. "Also, you'll need to rent our bowling shoes. Can't wear those you got on."

"I don't think we're ready for ordering a special ball, but we'll rent the shoes," remarked Phyl. "Maybe you could help us find the lightest balls on the racks." "Sure," said the young man as he proceeded to lift various bowling balls from the nearest lanes. "Not any of these. Let's try the next lane." He had searched several lanes before he found a couple we could use.

"This is still heavy," I said to Phyl. "But I guess it is the best he has."

"Mine is heavy too, but we'll make do." We put on the rented shoes and asked the couple playing in the next lane to refresh our memories on how to keep score. After an uneventful game of bowling, we began our walk back to Jesse Lee Home and the staff cottage. Laughingly Phyllis commented, "Don't think anyone in Seward will be contacting us to play in a bowling league soon."

"Nor will we be ordering our own special light weight balls any time in the future," I laughed. It was a pleasant walk with the clouds coming and going, allowing the sun to appear now and then. We exchanged stories of our lives, as we walked and continued to build a bond of friendship. "Seward sure is pretty on a day like this," I commented.

"Yes, a beautiful day brings the beauty out in Seward, but on rainy days, it can be a drab picture. Shall we stop in the office and check our mail?"

As we entered the building and turned to our left to enter the office door, Dolores came out carrying a large package, grinning from ear to ear.

"Well, what's this, Dolores? Last I looked on the calendar, it wasn't Christmas," commented Phyllis.

"Oh, hi there, Phyllis and Betty Jane. Good day off?"

"Great. Phyllis has been showing me the town. We went bowling."

"Oh, Kyle tries to get me in there now and then. I'm not very good. The balls are probably too heavy anyway."

"They are!" Phyl and I responded in unison.

"Whatcha got in that package, Dolores?" I asked.

"It's another family size mixer. The women in one of the churches in Washington sent it up. Thought I'd leave it in the staff kitchen in this building. You girls can use it sometime, if you like."

"You mean like cook?" laughed Phyllis. "No, thanks. I'll leave that to you *regular* housemothers. I have enough work just keeping the kids in line as a relief housemother. After we get the mail, we're going over to the kitchen to see what *Mrs. Echols has cooked* and will let us take to the cottage for supper. Nope, not cooking."

"As you wish," smiled Dolores, as she headed toward the Boys Building.

"Now, B.J., we can eat in the dining room with the rest tonight, if you like, but I prefer to get something from the kitchen and eat in the cottage. What is your wish?"

"That's fine. Let's warm something up in the cottage. Then we can spend the rest of the evening reading or answering these letters. I got three," I said jubilantly. "Did you get any?"

"Yes, one. But it's from my sister and doesn't need a quick reply."

"Of course, if you've arranged a couple of hot dates for us tonight . . . ."

"I wish. Afraid not but there *is* a record player in the cottage, and I have some good music we can listen to, while we relax and fortify ourselves for the kids being home *all day* tomorrow."

"Ya know, I've been thinking," I remarked as we started walking towards the arcade leading to the kitchen. "Poor Mrs. Bloom. She has those D Boys *all day* every day but her one day off. Does she ever get a break?"

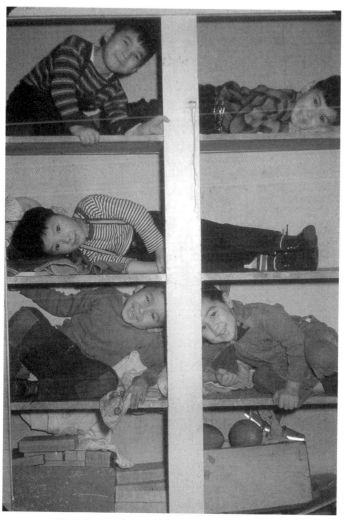

The D Boys at play. Photo from Rachel Yokel's collection.

179

"Not during the day, but as you have noticed, she puts those little boys to bed right after dinner, and that gives her peace and quiet every evening, more or less. She also puts them down for a rest time on their beds after lunch. Some actually fall asleep. Rachel has spoken of spending some time with the little boys in a kindergarten session, maybe three mornings a week. That would help."

"Does Rachel want you to assist her?"

"She hasn't asked."

"I was supposed to have that dorm, ya know. But the Blooms came along right before I arrived, and Mr. Matthews gave the D Boys to them. I was disappointed, but now that I'm beginning to see all of the time they require from a housemother, I think that was a lucky stroke for me."

"You better believe it! They pulled me over from the Girls Building once or twice to take care of the little boys briefly. I was never so glad to get back to the Girls Building! Only one of the little girls is as young as the D Boys. That's Leona."

"Then I will resent the Blooms no more."

* * *

Saturday morning I was startled by the usual loud clanging of the wake-up bell and immediately knew I was back in my room in the Boys Building. *Will I ever get used to that forever rude awakening sound? I'd better get up. Some of the boys will be eager to get the Saturday cleaning out of the way and will start before breakfast.* Sure enough, when I went into the dorm, some of the boys had stripped their beds and piled their dirty sheets in the middle of the floor. They knew that after breakfast, some of the big A Boys would deliver clean sheets and collect the big pile of soiled bed linens in the middle of the dorm floor and stuff them inside the huge laundry bags. The strongest of the A Boys were assigned to carry the huge bags to the pick-up truck that would be parked outside the front door of the building. One of the maintenance men would then drive the truck loaded with the big bags of soiled sheets and towels to the near-by TB San for laundering. It was a weekly event, and everyone had their own role in making sure the soiled linens were ready for leaving the building after breakfast each Saturday morning.

"Lookee here, Miss Epps! I got my sheets off, and I'm half way through cleaning out my drawers!" exclaimed Carl.

"So I see."

"He got up before the bell rang!" added Dale in disgust.

"Yeah, you woke us up," complained Jeff.

"Yeah, you did!" added his brother. It seemed the twins were always supporting each other, regardless of the matter.

"Floyd did too," said Carl, not willing to take all of the blame.

"Yeah, but I saw *you* get up first," was Floyd's comeback.

"Never mind. It's done, and we can't undo it. Carl and Floyd, I know you are eager to get your Saturday chores done, so you'll have more time to play, but you must be more considerate of the other boys who are still sleeping. So, don't let this happen again. Everybody up and out for breakfast! Try to strip your beds before the breakfast bell rings."

"Mis Sepps, will you check my drawers? I'm done," announced Floyd.

I walked over to check the early morning work of Floyd. I opened the drawer and saw clothing neatly organized. Someone has taught this six year old well, I thought. "Good job, Floyd! Let's see the other drawer." I opened the second drawer as Floyd's big, dark brown eyes beamed at approval of his work. His round fat cheeks moved outward into a smile.

"That one is good too, huh?"

"Yes, Floyd, this one is good too. You'll be all ready to put clean sheets on your bed, when a couple of A Boys bring them over this morning. Good work."

"Mine is *almost* through," said Carl.

"I'm not doin' my drawers 'til after breakfast," said Dale.

"Me neither!" said the twins in unison.

As most of the boys were leaving the dorm, I called after them, "When you are through washing up this morning, be sure to leave this week's towels on the bathroom floor by the door." I wondered why I even bothered to say that, since this had been the routine of these boys long before I arrived. Suddenly the answer came.

"Miss Epps, Floyd left his towel on the hook," said Kurt, returning from the bathroom. Although Kurt was the older and appeared more mature than some of the others, he wasn't above reporting the shortcomings of his dorm mates. He knew the rules. He had been at the Home longer than some of the rest, and he knew he was within his rights to report when a rule was broken. The others respected him and knew that Kurt played fair.

"Uh oh," said Floyd. "I forgot. I'll go get it," and he raced out of the big room.

Chuck shouted after him, "If you hadn't tried to get ahead of everybody this morning, maybe you wouldn't have forgot!" Chuck was voicing the resentment of everybody, who had awakened earlier than they were ready to crawl out of bed. Floyd was a newcomer to the dorm, and with Chuck's seniority, I guess he figured that gave him the right to call a bad play on the younger ones, without being labeled a squealer. In recent discussions with other staff, I learned that there seemed to exist some unwritten law that established a pecking order in each of the dorms. Without any orientation, the boys in each of the four dorms just seemed to fall in line and accept this fact. I found this an interesting phenomenon but knew I must make sure the older ones, as well as those with seniority, did not take advantage of their position.

* * *

Mr. Echols' son, Malvin, came to me after breakfast in the dining room saying, "Miss Epps, here is a box of tacks my Dad said for me to give you. He apologizes, and says he got busy and forgot to get them to you. He said to tell you he's sorry. He's started work already and asked me to give 'em to you."

"That's all right, Malvin. I understand. He is a busy man. Thank you. Now I can finish tacking the skirt around the radiator!" Malvin knew the smile on my face forgave his Dad for any procrastination. That child eats well for a twelve year old, I thought. If that keeps up, he is going to be a *big* man. Malvin seemed to get along with the other children and thus far, I had heard no complaints about him. He owned the only bicycle on the grounds and was probably the envy of many. I had no idea how much he shared with the others. There were no bicycle trails in existence in Seward, and sharing the rocky roads with traffic would neither be safe nor pleasurable biking.

Back in the C Dorm the boys had all stripped the beds, and the large pile of dirty linens in the middle of the floor was awaiting the A Boys. I checked the Saturday chores, as each of the boys reported his job was finished. Unlike Floyd and Carl, most of the boys waited until their Saturday chore was completed before reorganizing their drawers, except for the twins. This month they were the dorm sweepers and needed the pile of bed linens out of the way to do their job. By now all of the boys knew the expectations of a passable drawer, and few needed to do the job over. Housemothers usually checked for cleanliness, neatness, and no hidden rocks and debris from the beaches. In short time, a couple of A Boys came into the dorm followed by John Street.

"Hey, Miss Epps, got some dirty bed clothes for us?" asked John.

Max saw them approach and uninhibitedly, gave a running jump and landed on the big pile of laundry. "You gotta take me with it!"

"Me too!" said Floyd, not wanting to be left out of any fun. He joined Max on the laundry with a "Whoopee!"

"Here I come!" said Willy. Soon there was a pile-up of little boys on the laundry laughing and rolling on and off of the sheets. The A Boys were eager to play "King of the Hill" and to use their long arms to shove the young boys off the bed clothes.

"Yeah, you boys take care of that disturbance, while I talk to Miss Epps," said John, knowing full well the big boys would enjoy showing off their advantage of strength to these younger ones. I stared in amazement at the chaos in the middle of the floor. "Don't worry about it, Betty Jane. The big boys will make short order of that mischief. Just wanted to drop by and tell you that I'm flying home next weekend. So how about that date you promised me? Friday night okay? That *is* your day off isn't it?"

"Yes. But John, you are leaving so soon?!"

"Well, I've been here since spring. Time to move on. The books are calling me." The noise of the loud play was growing to an unacceptable level. "Hey!" shouted John. "Knock it off! We've got a schedule to meet."

John's big masculine, booming voice brought a momentary stop to the rough play, giving me a chance to step in with my housemother role.

"That's enough, boys! John needs to get on to other dorms and pick up their laundry. Help these A Boys get these sheets into the big bag." The boys knew this rowdy fun was coming to an end and obediently began to shove sheets into the huge bag.

"That's okay, Miss Epps, we can do it faster without their help," responded Roger, one of the big boys. I learned Roger's self esteem shot up when he made the high school varsity basket ball team, but not all of the younger boys realized how special was this achievement.

"We don't wanna help you anyway. You're too rough," pouted Ben.

"Oh, you a cry baby?" taunted Roger.

"I'm not crying!" snapped Ben.

"You're not laughin'," grinned Roger.

"Okay, get on with it guys. I've got to get the truck back to Mr. Bloom. He needs it for something." And then to me he added, "Friday it is?"

"Sure, John. That's fine."

John and the two A Boys left the dorm with the huge bag on Roger's back, and the other boy saying, "I get the next one, Roger. You've carried two in a row."

"You're not big enough to carry a heavy load," Roger taunted his working companion good naturedly.

"You wanna bet?!" came the reply.

John, sensing conflict arising said, "Okay, Daniel, you can carry the next two from the Girls Building."

"Nyah, nyah, nyah, nyah, nyah!" taunted Daniel to Roger.

"I told you guys! Knock it off! We don't have time for this." demanded John, as they walked down the hall towards the front door.

The thought occurred to me, *Guess I'm not the only one who has to step in when a conflict is brewing.*

Shoe polishing would take up some time after lunch, but I knew the boys had learned to do that quickly and would sandwich that into their play. I hoped the rain would stop sprinkling, so I could send the boys outdoors. There seemed to be less squabbling as they played in the great outdoors, than in the back playroom. I wondered if I should take up the project of tacking up the radiator curtain in the afternoon, or just wait until Monday, when the boys would be back in school. It seemed one of the boys always needed my input on something that couldn't wait, and that meant being called away from my task time and time again. That thought settled it. I'd wait until Monday.

Chapter 12

REVENGE—A CHOPPED OFF
FINGER—AND A NAKED PREACHER

The next morning at breakfast, Dolores leaned over the two small children sitting between us and asked, "How's that grapefruit, Betty Jane?"

"Very good," I replied. "It's nice to have fresh fruit so far north."

"No, I mean how is your grapefruit cut?"

"Across the center of the fruit."

"May I see?" Dolores got up from her place at the table to stand behind my chair. Peering at the grapefruit halves around the table, she shook her head saying, "They've done it again. I wonder who got the other half of my grapefruit that is cut the wrong way," and she glanced around the room.

"What do you mean?" I asked.

Dolores returned to her chair and lifted her grapefruit half, so I could see it. "See? It's cut the wrong way . . . lengthwise. I can't possibly dig the fruit out this way."

"Oh dear. Someone has made a mistake."

"Oh no! It's no mistake. You notice all of the other halves are cut the right way . . . crosswise. You can just bet some A Boy or A Girl is watching this scene with amusement. They expect me to struggle to get the fruit out of the rind. They think it's a big joke." About that time Dolores noticed that Phyllis was up from her table and walking toward the kitchen carrying a grapefruit half. "Ahhh, there's the other half of my grapefruit. Phyllis is taking her half back to the kitchen. I will too," and off she went following Phyllis.

Mrs. Echols apologized profusely, and said she tried to keep an eye on the big kids helping her prepare breakfast, but sometimes they sneaked something by her.

"Oh, don't worry about it, Mrs.Echols. It's just pay back time for a good scolding I gave some A Girls last night at the movies. I have an idea who did it, but they won't own up to this mischief," declared Phyllis.

"Well, hey! I wasn't at the movies! Why *me*?" asked Dolores.

"Because *someone* has to have the other half of my grapefruit, and it was probably your turn, Dolores. Don't think you were the one they were getting back at."

"I'm not so sure. This is not the first time this has happened to me."

"Well, I'll have Mr. Matthews talk to these kitchen helpers if they keep this up," responded Mrs. Echols. She went to the big refrigerator in the food storage room behind the kitchen and came back with a whole grapefruit. Mrs. Echols then proceeded to cut it the correct way. "There! That should make eating a little easier."

Both Dolores and Phyllis exchanged their grapefruits for the two halves offered by Mrs. Echols.

"Actually, it *is* kind of funny," chuckled Phyllis. "But I won't let them know that." Immediately she changed her facial expression to one of sedateness and walked back to the huge dining area. She knew which A Girls to eye but chose to ignore them completely.

"Ahhh, now I can eat," said Dolores returning to the table.

"You got another one, Miss Morey?" asked one of the C Girls at her table.

"I sure did. I'll show that culprit who cut my grapefruit the wrong way. I'm not about to struggle with eating the other one."

"Who was it?" asked the same child.

"I'll probably never know. They'll keep it a secret." Shortly thereafter, the entire dining room population was dismissed.

"All of us in the Boys Building are picked up first for Sunday School," Dolores reminded me, as we walked back to our dorms. "Did Rachel tell you?"

"Yes. We all go down in the big yellow bus?"

"Yes."

Soon I was glancing around the bus, and noticed that all of the boys, as well as my C Boys, were dressed in their finest and so was the staff. Once on the lagoon road, the bus began to bump and bounce up and down from the rough ride. It didn't seem to matter how slowly Mr. Bloom drove the bus, or how carefully he dodged the potholes, the ride was still a challenge to stay in one's seat comfortably. "How do you like this ride?" asked Dolores with a grin.

"It's a bit rough. Does it ever get any better?" I responded.

"Not since I've been here."

Arriving at the church, Mr. Bloom opened the door of the bus, and all of the boys seemed to know exactly what to do. They filed off of the bus and went up the steps of the little white church, passing by the sign that read "Seward Memorial Methodist Church, Rev. Charles Malin, Minister." Walking into the sanctuary, they moved into pews without being directed and sat quietly. They did not spread out over the sanctuary but stayed with their own dorm groups. The eleven C Boys took up one whole pew, as did the D Boys sitting behind them.

C Boys sitting in pew in Seward Methodist Church waiting for Sunday School to begin.

"We sit here and wait until the bus comes back with the girls. Then the group is dismissed to go to Sunday School classes in the basement," Dolores informed me.

I was somewhat surprised and certainly impressed with this scene of well disciplined behavior. "They all look downright angelic in their Sunday finery," I whispered to Dolores.

Dolores chuckled, "Don't they though! You wouldn't know these are the same boys we live with seven days a week."

"I should have brought my camera. This is *not* a common sight with all of them sitting there so quietly with every hair in place and in their Sunday best."

As soon as the girls arrived, the boys turned and looked toward their house parents, waiting for the nod that said they could leave their seats and go downstairs.

"The adult Sunday School class meets in the choir loft. Come, I'll show you. Oh, here comes Rev. Malin." A young, handsome minister was walking towards us.

"You must be the new housemother at Jesse Lee Home," he remarked to me.

"Yes, she is," said Dolores. "Rev. Malin, this is Betty Jane Epps. She is the new house mother for the C Boys."

He extended his hand as he said, "Welcome to Seward and welcome to our church."

"Thank you, I'm happy to be here."

"We're glad to have you." And then to Dolores he said, "I missed last Wednesday because I was out of town, but tell the boys I'll be out for basketball practice this Wednesday night."

"I'll tell them. They miss you when you don't come."

"Well, tell them sometimes it just can't be helped," and he moved on to greet others.

"He comes out once a week and coaches the A and B Boys in basketball," Dolores explained.

"Do they play against each other or other teams from town?"

"Practice is against each other, but sometimes they play other teams in town. Some of the A Boys play on the high school basketball team, too."

Rev. Charles Malin and the Jesse Lee Home Basket Ball team. Photo from Rachel Yokel's collection.

"Are there that many teams in town to compete with?"

"Oh basketball is big in this town, and *everybody* turns out for the high school games, they tell me. I'm not that much into it, but Kyle keeps me informed."

By now we had reached the choir area, and I was introduced to the pleasant, middle-aged teacher, Mr. Blanchard. I noticed that the Jesse Lee Home staff outnumbered the townspeople in attendance in the class. It was a typical Methodist Sunday School class with the lesson coming from a scripture reading and discussion following. Between Sunday School and church, I was able to chat briefly with a few of the town folk in the class, but after the church service, there was no time to get to know anybody. The bus left almost immediately with the boys, and Sunday mid-day dinner was ready, as soon as the second bus load returned.

These meals following the church service were very special indeed, for almost always fried chicken was on the menu; and definitely there was ice cream that had been made in hand freezers the night before. The A Boys took turns cranking the handles.

After preparing these much appreciated mid-day Sunday dinners, the cook was given *every* Sunday afternoon off. That meant the big kids prepared sandwiches for the evening meal. Since these were put into paper bags with a piece of fruit and a cookie, the prepared food could be used for picnics in good weather. Often the dorms took advantage of these sack meals and went for long walks in the Seward area: into the woods, to the city park at First Lake, or to the beaches of Resurrection Bay. The four oldest dorm groups took a turn about one Sunday per month and prepared these mobile suppers.

The sun was shining brightly on this particular Sunday afternoon. So I stepped outside the front door of the Boys Building simply to feel the sunshine on my face for a few moments. To my surprise, Dolores was there calling to some of her boys.

"Hello, Dolores. What's up? Are you out here enjoying the sunshine too?"

"Oh, I wish! No, it's my dorm's turn to prepare the Sunday supper, and I am out here rounding up my boys to help me."

"And what surprises will you and your boys be putting in those paper sacks tonight? Anything special?"

"Not very. It seems to me that when our turn comes, more often than not, one of my least favorite foods is on the menu . . . cold sliced beef heart."

"I don't know that I've ever had it. You don't recommend it, huh?"

"Oh, I don't mind the taste so much as the preparation. Only a staff person can use the automatic electric meat slicer. I would prefer spreading ground cooked moose on sandwiches but instead, I've got to use that menacing machine to slice the beef heart. One hundred slices at least!" And in despair she added, "What have I done to deserve this?"

By this time more of the B Boys were gathering around Dolores and Maurice said, "It's not you, Miss Morey, it was Ella Mae."

"Ella Mae? What do you mean?" Dolores asked.

"Yeah," chuckled Clyde. "Wouldn't that have been somethin' to see!"

"They said she was drippin' blood everwhere!" chimed in Horace. "I'd like to have seen that!" he added with glee.

"What are you talking about?" asked Dolores.

"When Ella Mae chopped her finger off in the meat slicin' machine!" said Maurice. No doubt Dolores and I *both* had visions of that chaotic drama dancing in our heads. "That's why us kids can't use the machine any more. Just housemothers can use it."

"Why that's awful! When did this repulsive scene happen?" I asked.

"Last year!" all of the boys chimed in.

"Yeah, and Harriet found it," said Clyde continuing the story.

"Found it?" responded Dolores.

"The finger!" said the boys in unison. This story was becoming more gruesome by the second, and I could tell the boys were enjoying creating this gross scene for Dolores and my benefit. Yet, somehow I didn't think they were making it all up.

"Mr. Matthews and Miss Dolliver came back to look for it," said Clyde.

"Back from where?" asked Dolores, realizing she was having to put this story in some order, as their comments were called out to her.

"The hospital!" they all responded.

"The doctor wanted to sew it back on," said Maurice.

"They were lookin' everywhere in the kitchen for it, when Harriet came in and asked what they were lookin' for," added Horace.

"Yeah," chuckled Clyde. "She had it all along. She took it out of the garbage, where someone had thrown it."

I could tell Dolores was about ready to gag at the thought, and the boys beamed with even more pride.

"Miss Dolliver told Harriet she was a hero for saving the finger, and they rushed it down to the hospital," said Maurice concluding the story.

"Yeah, she was lucky. Huh, Miss Morey?" remarked Horace.

"Well, I guess so if the surgeon was successful in reattaching her finger. How much of her finger did she lose?" asked Dolores looking down at her own hands that were about to be subjected to the possibility of the same fate.

"It was the tip of her finger," replied Horace.

Dolores looked at me and said, "Somehow I have to erase this story from my mind, if I am to accomplish this task of preparing the evening meal."

"Good luck!" I replied.

She took a deep breath. "All right, enough of that story. We've got a meal to prepare. Let's go to the kitchen." She began to dole out responsibilities to individual boys, as they headed back into the building.

"If you've got a minute, Betty Jane, come on over to the kitchen and I'll show you this fearful machine."

My curiosity was up. "I'll see what I can arrange." I went to the C Boys' playroom and told the few playing there that I'd be over in the dining area with Miss Morey, and if anyone needed me, I'd be back in about ten minutes.

When I arrived in the kitchen, Dolores was standing in front of the slicing machine holding a large chunk of meat. Seeing me appear, she laughed nervously saying, "You can see that I am approaching this task with guarded fear and trepidation. I keep telling myself the horrid story is just giving me more thought for caution."

"Of course. That's the attitude," was my encouraging reply.

She told me she had read all of the cautionary statements printed on the machine. "But I can't put the slicing off any longer. So here goes." She flipped the switch, and even the sound of the machine was menacing. We watched as the sharp, circular blade rolled forward round and round ready to receive the chunk of meat. Again she forced a laugh saying, "I *will* rise above this fear!" And indeed she did! She showed those boys she could handle that machine in spite of their story. I knew it wasn't easy for her. As the first slices fell from the large chunk of meat and she still had her fingers, Dolores began to smile. Yes, she was handling this task quite well. The boys had been denied any more talk of Ella Mae and the chopped off finger, so they began to fill each of the one hundred paper bags with a cookie, an orange, and a carrot. I congratulated Dolores and returned to my dorm.

After the sandwiches were made, Dolores and her boys let the dorms know that our Sunday evening meal was ready.

As the C Boys and I filed into the dining room to take a sack dinner from the distribution counter, Mack asked, "Miz Sepps, can we have supper on the beach?"

"Where on the beach?" I replied.

"Just right down there. Miz Yokel takes us there lots of times."

If Rachel took them, I had to assume it was okay.

"Yeh," said Jeff. "Let's go down to the ship wreck."

"Yeh, Miss Epps, there's a big boat down there that was wrecked. It's still there," added his twin brother Jack. "Can we go?" Others were chiming in with the same requests.

"We can walk down there?" I inquired.

"Sure!" "We've done it lots of times!" "Miss Yokel took us!" came the simultaneous remarks.

"All right. Let's go back to the dorm and get our jackets." The boys began to move with haste and full of glee, as though I had granted them a very special gift.

"Luck-eeeeeee!" they called to others, as they gathered at the front door of the Boys Building. "We're going to the beach!"

We walked down the gravel road toward Resurrection Bay staying away from the main highway. It was a beautiful day with the Arctic sun still beaming down on us. I thought this would be pleasant for all. Tennessee had no beaches except around lakes, so this would be a new adventure for me. Once we reached the highway crossing that would take us to the beach, I corralled the eleven boys and we crossed the thoroughfare together. I insisted they stay together until we all reached the beach. Then they would be free to spread out.

The "wrecked ship" turned out to be one end of a discarded old fishing boat that the boys loved crawling all over and exploring. When they tired of this, they began to slowly spread out over the beach to look for shells and poke through the washed up debris for something of interest. It was very windy by the water, and it smelled of the sea and the life it contained. I was glad I had insisted they all bring jackets, although the boys were used to the sudden drops in the Alaskan temperatures when the winds came up. They felt no need to keep something on their arms as I did.

I suspected a beef heart sandwich would not become a preference of mine, but having dinner out of a paper bag was fun, regardless of its contents. After a while, the fascination of the beach was wearing off, and some of the boys began to bicker with each other. It was time to return.

* * *

In the middle of the week, Rev. Malin showed up at one of the tables in the dining room. "Looks like we have a guest for dinner," I remarked to Dolores. "I see the minister is here."

"Oh, he's here for dinner almost every Wednesday night. He does the vespers following the evening meal. When he isn't here, we take turns."

"Ahhhh, something I'll be asked to do in the future?"

"Oh, yes. We wouldn't want to leave you out," she chuckled. "We make it brief because of the attention span and try to offer something that is beneficial to the wide age range."

"That's quite an order."

"Yes, but you'll probably get a chance to observe several staff doing vespers, before they call on you to bring us some inspirational thoughts to ponder." Our conversation was interrupted, as all heads bowed for the blessing delivered by Rev. Malin. Then the hustle and bustle of distributing the food on the tables began.

"He's also here to coach the boys in basketball after dinner," remarked Dolores.

"That's right. Last Sunday he did say he would be here. I remember that. That should please your boys."

"Oh yes!" she answered and then paused before she continued. "This is my night off, so if any B Boy gets clobbered by running into a wall or whatever, Rachel will have to take care of it."

"So what are you going to do tonight?"

"Kyle is picking me up after dinner, and we're going to the Melroys for dessert. So I'm going to pass up these brownies tonight."

"They have chocolate in them. Are you sure you can do that, Dolores?"

"Oh, I've thought ahead. I'll be taking one of these little delights back to my room to consume, when I need my spirits raised at some point in the future."

"Always thinking, Dolores. That's what I like about you."

"Well, one must when one is in the frozen North, where chocolate stores do not abound to handle one's habit." Suddenly dinner was over, and Rev. Malin was reading scripture to the room. He followed with a simple story to illustrate the Bible reading, and vespers was over.

Dolores smiled, "That was short tonight. Guess he's as eager as the boys to get on the basketball court."

Wednesday was also shower night, and that meant starting the C Boys on their showers before the 7:00 p.m. bed time. I discovered that the boys didn't mind Wednesday and Saturday night showers. For some it was very much play time. Rachel had recommended checking each one before they got into clean pajamas, because some were less thorough than others. In the past, Rachel made sure they had washed their hair and especially their knees and elbows, where the summer soil often lingered. I could handle that, so one by one, as each boy left the bathroom, arms, legs, and wet heads were extended from their bathrobes for my inspection. During this process, I discovered that the native American coloring varied in shades of darkness, especially around the knees and elbows. It seemed the boys with the darkest knees were also those who enjoyed playing in the dirt. When in doubt, I sent them back to do it again. "That's not dirt, Mis Sepps. That's just me!" was the usual response. I soon discovered that sending one back to the showers usually resulted in the volume of noise being raised in the bathroom, and soon one would come running out tattling on the others.

"Dem boys are climbing on the shower stalls!" complained Willy. "And Ben snapped his towel on my back side!"

Although they were young boys, I tried to honor their privacy and stay out of the steamy shower room, but sometimes conflicts demanded that I stick my head through the door. The first time revealed a scene of boys playing chase on the wet floor and dodging snapping towels aimed at any convenient place on their naked bodies. Much to my surprise, boys were literally climbing to the top of the shower stalls to gain a better position to deliver the sting of the towel. Raising my voice above the shouts and laughter in this chaos, I delivered an ultimatum. "Everybody out and dressed for bed in ten minutes or *no story!*" I learned that usually did it, because the boys loved story time. For one thing it extended the 7:00 p.m. bed time. That hour was simply too early for some of them. They weren't ready to settle down and go to sleep. At one point I asked Rachel, "Why do the boys go to bed so early? My nieces and nephews are younger than these boys, and they don't go to bed this early."

"It's always been this way at Jesse Lee, Betty Jane . . . that I know of. Institutional living requires strict schedules, and thus far, it works. Yes, they complain, but they play hard, and nine to nine-and-a-half hours bed rest keeps them healthy for the most part."

Although it was tough on some of the boys, I discovered that it was very nice for tired housemothers. Very soon I began to appreciate that early hour. After 7:00 p.m. became *my* time for *my* needs, and the quiet of the evening was a welcome respite from the demands of eleven little boys all day long. There was no television to relax with in 1952, nor did I have a radio. But I did have a record player and some records of Broadway musicals that gave me much listening pleasure. However, on this particular night, I wanted to get started ironing some of those white shirts I had laundered on Monday. I went to my sewing room and set up the ironing board to begin this task. I knew there would be no interruptions, because the C Boys were asleep. If any disturbance arose in the dorm, I would hear that more readily from the sewing room than from my room. About half way through the ironing, suddenly Dolores appeared.

"I followed the music and sure enough I found you." Her face was beet red.

"Hello, Dolores. What's up? You look flushed."

"No doubt I do. I have just experienced the most embarrassing moment of my life!"

"What happened? Weren't you out with Kyle?"

"Oh, yes. He just dropped me off. It wasn't Kyle. It was Rev. Malin."

"Oh?"

"Well, you know he was here to play basketball with the boys, and he usually showers *with* the boys after the games. When I went upstairs, I knew the boys were in bed, but I heard the sound of water dripping from one of the showers in the B Boys' bathroom. I walked into the bathroom ready to turn off the shower faucet, when out stepped Rev. Malin naked as a jay bird!"

"Oh, Dolores! How embarrassing!"

"Tell me about it!" she said in agreement.

"What did he say?" I asked, beginning to be amused, yet feeling her distress.

"Nothing! I didn't give him a chance to say anything. I quickly turned on my heels, apologizing as I went exclaiming, 'Oh! I'm sorry. Excuse me!' I came right down here. I'm hiding out."

"So this just happened?"

"Yes. May I stay with you for awhile? I doubt he'll come down here looking for me, if he wants to comment."

"Fine. You can keep me company while I iron these last two shirts."

"And I'll enjoy the music with you. What's playing? Oklahoma?"

"Yes. I love this show." Conversation stopped as we both listened to the music. Dolores was no doubt trying to erase the recent incident from her mind, and I pondered what could be said to relieve some of the stress she was feeling. Finally I said, "You know, Dolores, he *is* married and probably is less bothered by all this than you are."

"Well, let's hope. I don't know how I'll keep a straight face Sunday morning, when he's preaching in the pulpit, and all I can see is his exit from the shower stall." We both laughed, and then immediately attempted to stifle the sound, so the C Boys would not be awakened. "Maybe Mr. Matthews will let me attend another church on Sunday mornings. Next Sunday is my Sunday off, and you can bet I won't be sitting in Seward Memorial Methodist Church!" Again we laughed.

"Ahhh, at last! My *last* shirt!"

"Ya know, I don't iron shirts."

"Do your boys do their own?"

"No, an angel does them."

"Where do you get one of those? I want one."

"I met her at an outing with Kyle. She became interested in me, because I work at Jesse Lee. Asked me all about it and asked how she could help."

"And you said, 'Come do my ironing?'"

"Actually I did but in a joking way. Much to my surprise, she showed up on ironing day shortly thereafter and took over my ironing board."

"Who is she? A sweet little old lady?"

"No, she's my age and without children. I think they live in a trailer somewhere down town. I call her 'my angel'."

"And rightly so. As the C Boys say, 'Luck-eeeeee!' "

Chapter 13

EMBARRASSMENT CITY AND A SNEAKY FIRE DRILL

I seated myself in front of Mr. Matthews' desk in the office.

"Morning, 'Tennessee,' what can I do for you?"

I began with my well rehearsed speech, "I have to tell you something."

"Something going wrong in the C Dorm?"

"No, it's not the boys. It's me."

"From what I hear, you're doing a fine job over there. What's the problem?"

I was wishing he'd stop interrupting. I was trying to focus on just how to tell this in such a way that would leave the least question about my personal behavior. "I need to tell you about something that happened on my way to Jesse Lee Home. I may need your help."

Elwin Matthews suddenly became very curious. "What's that, Betty Jane?"

"Rev. McGinnis, the Methodist minister in Juneau, suggested I tell you about this and let you take care of it."

"And?"

I began to tell my new employer about the middle-aged waiter who insisted I remain at his table when my U. S. Coast Guard friends got off the *Aleutian* in Ketchikan. I followed with revealing the "love letter" I had received at the Baranof Hotel, that had been hand carried by someone from the ship. I spoke of my shock in receiving that, and insisted nothing in my behavior had warranted a proposal of marriage. I knew the *Aleutian* would be docking in Seward soon, and the letter said he would meet up with me in Seward for my answer. "If the letter is not a hoax played on him by his friends . . . and I have no way of knowing this, will you cut him off at the door? I have no desire to see this man. I am hoping, if he shows up, he will come to the office first and not to the Boys Building."

"Don't you worry about it, Betty Jane. I'll take care of it." I was relieved that he asked no further questions. If the waiter ever came to Jesse Lee, I knew nothing about it. Neither I nor Mr. Matthews ever mentioned it again. So eventually, I assumed it may have been a joke the other waiters were playing on their friend.

Returning to the Boys Building, I climbed the stairs to the second floor to drop in on Dolores. Her door was open. "Hi, Dolores, what are you doing?"

Holding up a pair of jeans, Dolores replied, "No matter how many times I remind them to empty their pockets before putting their pants in the laundry, it is always an adventure going through their jeans. Look at this." Spread out on the floor was a collection of odds and ends that would probably interest only boys: a long rusty nail, the stub from a ticket to a recent movie, a marble, an array of rocks, the casing from a bullet, the hair from some wild animal (probably found in the woods), a fishing lure, and a broken pencil. "And I have four more pairs of jeans to go through. Will they ever learn?"

"My! That's quite a collection! Ever find anything useful?"

"Not to me."

"Well, I mustn't keep you from your task."

"No problem. This is an easy one compared to the next one on my list."

"And what might that be?"

"Some of the boys have joined a Boy Scout troop in town. I want them to look as well as the town kids, but these uniforms have been handed down from one boy to the other so many times, some are in ill repair."

I walked over to Dolores' bed and picked up several Boy Scout scarves that I spied while she was talking. "Well, these look brand new," I commented.

"They are. They came in yesterday's mail. Some folks are sending me money from back home, and I'm using the money to add one brand new item to each uniform as I can."

"That must please the boys."

"Oh, they are delighted to have something about their uniform that no one else has ever worn before."

"Well, those scarves will certainly spruce up a uniform."

"They help. But I wish I had a magic wand to wave over some of these tired uniforms to freshen them up more."

"At the rate you are going, you'll have your boys equal in appearance to any of the town Boy Scouts."

"I'm trying," she called after me, as I left the room.

The next day when the last C Boy was out the door for school, I took advantage of the fact I was alone and took a long hot shower to wash my hair. Stepping out of the shower, I wrapped a towel around my full head of red hair to absorb as much moisture as I could. Then I stared into the mirror at my clean, young face and reminded myself . . . you are a very 'plain jane' without the help of make-up. *Yep, you need some color in your face, Miss Betty.* With the towel still wrapped around my head, I slipped into clean clothing, when suddenly there was a knock on my door. "Just a minute. I'm coming," I called. I opened the door, and much to my surprise stood the handsome purser from the *Aleutian* in uniform with three or four people in tow.

"Hello, there. Remember me?" and then he began to laugh.

"Oh, my goodness! Look how you have caught me. I just got out of the shower!" And he responded with more laughter.

"Well, you said on the *Aleutian* that I could bring passengers up from the ship who wanted to see Jesse Lee Home, and you would give us a tour."

"I did indeed, but I'm sorry you've caught me like this." He laughed even more heartily.

Introductions were made, and his passengers apologized that they hadn't called ahead.

"We stopped at the office, and they said to come on over to this building and told us where we could find you," said the purser.

"Well, if you don't mind going on the tour as you've found me, I'll be happy to keep my word."

"We'll wait while you take the towel off your head," the purser said, still chuckling. I knew the removal of the towel would not improve my appearance, as my hair was straight and needed some curlers to make me presentable.

"Nope. You get me just as I am, wet hair wrapped in a towel and plain face without any make-up."

"Oh, you look fine," one of the passengers politely offered and once again apologized. I knew that was a courtesy remark and not a word of truth in it. With my hair still wrapped in a towel, I led the group through the halls of the Boys Building, and then we went into the dining room. I answered the questions from the visiting passengers, as we moved along. Next we went up the stairs to the library. In the narrow staircase, the purser began to laugh again.

"What's so funny?" I asked.

"You!" he began with a big burst of laughter. "I told these folks about this beautiful young girl that I had met earlier on the ship with this beautiful red hair, and I was so looking forward to showing you off." He gave another big burst of laughter.

Obviously, there was no subtlety in that remark. His implication on the state of my appearance was as plain as the non-powdered nose on my face. At this point, my face flushed with embarrassment, and inside, I was seething with a degree of humiliation I had never experienced before. I knew without the enhancement of a little make-up, I was downright homely, but that was my secret. *How dare he expose this fact to the world!* Yet, I knew I must play the role of the gracious hostess for the sake of the Jesse Lee Home. "That's what you get for not calling ahead," I said, keeping my reddened face away from his sight.

The passengers supported me with their remarks: "Well, I should say." "Isn't it the truth!" "Maybe he'll learn something from this."

There was only one more building to go, and the ordeal would be over. Then this awful incident would become history. Soon they were saying their goodbyes to me and expressing thanks, as they exited the Girls Building. I fairly ran through the buildings back to my room to make myself presentable. I plopped myself down into a chair with a sigh and hoped I would never have to go through that again.

The next morning we were awakened at 6:00 a.m. by a horrendous ringing of the bell in a rhythmic pattern we had never heard before.

Suddenly the sound of running feet was everywhere, and Mrs. Bloom was shouting over the din of excitement and confusion, "Stop running! Stop running! It's only a fire drill!"

I grabbed my robe, and quickly went into my dorm finding the boys in various stages of reaction. Some were jumping up and down, as though it were a party, while others were sitting up in their beds with a look of confusion.

"Mis Sepps! What's happening?" yelled Willy.

"I believe it's a fire drill!" I yelled back, trying to raise my voice over the constant loud, rhythmic pattern of the bell. "Grab your robes and house slippers, and go out the front door and wait for me! There was a scurry of activity, as I began to go from bed to bed ushering the boys onto their feet.

"Hey! Look out the window!" yelled Chuck. "Everybody is out there!" Several boys ran to the windows.

"They're in their pajamas!" laughed Jeff.

"Hey, let me see!" said Jack elbowing his way to the windows.

I immediately moved to scatter the boys and point them on their way out of the dorm. "This is not a laughing matter! This is a practice in case there is a fire!"

"Fire? Is there a fire?" asked Dale, beginning to show signs of fright.

"No, it's a pretend fire! But we must get out of the building fast." Finally the last of my boys was out of the dorm, and I hurriedly followed.

Rachel was standing at the front door directing traffic, assuring the passing boys, who were moving with haste, "That's good! Let's move along quickly. It's *not* a fire! It's a fire drill."

Outside the building Mr. Bloom was calling, "Go to your house parent! Stand by your housemothers!"

A couple of my boys were trying to get his attention saying loudly, "She ain't here! Mis Sepps is not out here!"

Mr. Bloom looked over his shoulder and saw me exiting the building. "Here she comes. C Boys, go stay by Miss Epps!" To me he said, "Miss Epps, go down there away from the building. I'll send the C Boys to you!"

I moved in the direction to which he was pointing, passing by Dolores in her robe with her boys all gathered around her. I noticed Mrs. Bloom was fully dressed with her brood of little D Boys jumping up and down with excitement. A Boys and their two housemothers were still coming out of the building in two's and three's. I began to count as my boys ran towards me. In short time they were all there.

"Housemothers! Are all of your boys out of the building?" Female voices began to loudly return an answer in the affirmative. "Wait here," he instructed, "until I come back." He then disappeared into the building. Shortly thereafter the loud bell stopped its clanging, rhythmic pattern. Several, who had covered their ears with their hands, began to relax their arms.

"Boy! Dat was loud!" remarked Willy.

"Sure was," I responded.

Dolores, standing nearby with her group, called to me, "Surpriiise! Surprise!"

"Did you know this was coming?" I asked.

"They told us about it last night at the Bible study class. Didn't tell us when but said to warn our kids."

"No wonder your boys knew exactly what to do."

"No, I didn't get to prepare them. They were all bedded down and asleep when I got back from the study. They just weren't wide enough awake at 6:00 a.m. to challenge my demands this morning. As you can see, they didn't take time to grab their robes."

"Noooo. She wouldn't let us." "Couldn't even grab our shoes!" responded a couple of B Boys.

"Grumble. Grumble," mocked Dolores lightly laughing.

After noticing Mrs. Bloom bending over scolding one of her boys, I left my group momentarily and walked over to Dolores. In a soft voice I said to Dolores, "You notice Mrs. Bloom is the only housemother completely dressed."

Dolores chuckled, "Yes, I guess there is an advantage to sleeping with the 'fire marshal.' "

About that time, Mr. Bloom came out of the building speaking in a loud voice. "Okay! Thank you for exiting the building as fast as you did. You did well! But we'll have to try to be even faster next time. Now that you know what a fire drill is, we'll do better next time. You can go back in now." The groups began to disperse and move toward the entrance to the building.

"Oh, look," said Jeff, looking at the Girls Building. "The girls are out of their building, too."

"Well, of course," said Rachel walking to the C Boys. "You didn't think we'd leave the girls in their building to burn up, did you?"

"Was there a real fire?" asked Alvin.

"No, silly," said Jack. "It was just pretend. Wasn't it, Miss Yokel?"

"Yes, that's all that it was. But it's important to practice to get out of the building fast, so we'll know what to do in the event of a real fire." That comment seemed to satisfy the boys, and they proceeded to enter the building. To me, Rachel said, "I need to apologize to you, Betty Jane. I think you are the only one who hadn't been warned that a fire drill would be coming. I guess Mr. Bloom, having worked on merchant ships and knowing the importance of fire drills, was appalled when he asked Mr. Matthews how often we had drills. Mr. Matthews told him that we hadn't had any. So our superintendent has put Mr. Bloom in charge of drills. Some of us were just told last night and didn't expect one quite so soon."

"Why couldn't he have waited until we at least had a time to discuss proper procedure for emptying the building with the kids?" asked Dolores contributing to the conversation.

"That would have helped, but maybe he wanted to dramatize how unprepared we are, and that would improve our attitude about doing fire drills," responded Rachel.

"I would have gotten the point just as well without losing my last fifteen minutes of sleep this morning," replied Dolores.

"Oh, I agree!" I responded.

"Mr. Matthews asked me to prepare you, Betty Jane, since you didn't hear the announcement last night. When I returned to the Boys Building, you were already asleep.

"I confess I fell asleep reading. I'm sorry."

"That's okay. I understand." The three of us began to walk back into the building.

As we were entering the building, John Street was coming out and fully dressed. "Bet Mr. Bloom let *him* know about this sneaky fire drill," said Dolores.

Knowing I didn't look my best, I wanted to avoid a conversation with John.

"Good morning, ladies."

"Hi, John," said Rachel. "How did you like that surprise drill?"

"No surprise. I rang the bell," he grinned.

"I knew it!" said Dolores.

"Caught that porcupine yet?" asked Rachel.

"Yes. The critter's downfall was his taste for the creosote under the building. Betty Jane and I had southern fried porcupine the other night. He noticed that I was about to disappear into my room and called, "Betty Jane, tell them what great chefs we were!" They all laughed and went their separate ways to begin another day.

Chapter 14

PICNIC UNDER THE RAILROAD BRIDGE AND "AUTUMN - WHEN A YOUNG MAN'S FANCY TURNS . . ."

In the dining room on a late Sunday afternoon, the sack suppers were ready to be collected by those groups who wanted to picnic away from Jesse Lee. Yesterday's sprinkles had ceased, and the boys were clamoring to go for a walk and picnic under the *railroad bridge*.

"Yeah, Miss Epps, we'll show you where it is. It's down the highway," said Ben.

"The highway?" I asked cautiously.

"Yeah, Miss Yokel takes us there *all* the time," added Ben. I was beginning to wonder if the boys had figured out, if they added Rachel's okay to any request, their housemother usually said yes. All right, I'd get the exact location from Rachel and give it a try. It would give me a chance to see more of the surrounding area.

With Rachel's directions and all eleven of the boys corralled together for the walk down to the highway, we started down the front steps of the Boys Building and immediately noticed an approaching car. "It's Miss Morey!" shouted Floyd.

"Hi! Miss Morey!" shouted Ben as the car stopped. Then all of the boys joined in with a noisy greeting. Dolores smiled and waved at the group through the closed window. The door opened on the driver's side, and Kyle walked around to the passenger side to open the door for Dolores.

Well, I guess chivalry isn't dead in Alaska. I'm impressed. Kyle appears to be a true gentleman, I thought.

Kyle opened the door, and Dolores stepped out of the car still dressed in her best clothes for Sunday. "Hi, guys! Where are you going?" she asked. Several responses were offered at the same time.

"Down to the railroad bridge!"

C Boys having a Sunday supper picnic under the railroad bridge.

"Down to the highway."

"We're gonna eat under the railroad bridge."

"Gonna walk along the fishin' stream under the railroad tracks on the bridge."

"That should be fun. Taking Miss Epps with you, are you?"

I smiled knowing Dolores was well aware the boys had talked me into this outing.

"Yeah," said Floyd. "She gotta go. We can't go by ourselves. Mr. Matthews won't let us."

"Yeah," said Willy. "Dat's right."

"I think that's wise, boys. Mr. Matthews knows best." Dolores turned to Kyle. "Kyle, I'd like you to meet our newest member of the staff. This is Betty Jane Epps from Tennessee."

"How do you do?" responded the handsome, blonde, young man.

"I'm happy to meet you. I've heard nice things about you," I offered. Kyle looked at Dolores and smiled.

"Don't look at me," teased Dolores. "She must have been talking to someone else."

Kyle just grinned and let that pass. "So how do you like Alaska thus far?"

"It's beautiful."

"Yes, it is," smiled Kyle and he turned to look at the view of Resurrection Bay and Mt. Alice. "Newcomers are usually enthralled by our vast wilderness and all it has to offer."

I couldn't resist jumping in with the comment, "Yes, I hear some have been introduced to a little more of the wildlife than was bargained for."

Kyle responded with a questioned brow.

"I'm sure she's talking about the bear we met on the trail," prompted Dolores.

"Oh, yes. I didn't plan that trip very well, did I? I haven't gotten her out into the wilderness since."

"Well, you're doing it tonight. We're joining some folks having a wiener roast somewhere in the woods, Betty Jane. Believe me, I've thought twice about accepting this invitation."

"You gonna be eaten up by a bear, Miss Morey," teased Ben.

"Yeah!" chimed in some of the others.

"Thanks, boys. On that reassuring note, I'll pop upstairs and change into my campfire clothes. I wouldn't want the bear to eat my best Sunday dress."

"Oh, you're safe, Dolores. I hear wild animals don't like fire. Am I right, Kyle?" I added.

"That's right and I'll see that a roaring fire is kept burning!" assured Kyle.

Dolores was half way up the front steps of the building when she turned and said to Kyle, "You wait here by the car until I've changed. Betty Jane and the C Boys will keep you entertained."

"En . . . ner . . . tained? What's dat?" asked Willy.

"That means you have to do a tap dance for Miss Morey's boy friend!" giggled Ben.

"Not me. Yoooooou!" quickly responded Willy.

"I'm not gonna dance," Ben answered decisively. Changing the expression on his face to a big grin, he turned and looked up into Kyle's face, "You gonna kiss Miss Morey?" Some of the others chimed in with a like question.

"All right, boys. That's enough. Sorry about that Kyle," I interceded.

"I'm used to that from the B Boys. Doesn't bother me. So, you fellows are going under the railroad bridge, huh?"

"Yeah," chimed in Floyd, never wanting to be left out of any conversation. "It's fun!"

Dale, Alvin, and Kurt just stood by with grins on their faces, as did most of the others quietly watching the whole scene.

"Aren't you afraid a train will run over you?" asked Kyle. The three boys shook their heads indicating no.

"We're not going *on* the tracks, silly. We stay *under* the bridge," prompted Ben.

"Oh, well, I guess that is safe then."

"I certainly hope so. This will be my first opportunity to dine in Seward under the bridge with the C Boys," I declared.

"I think I know where they are talking about. If they stay *under* the tracks, they should be safe."

"We always stay *under* the tracks," added Chuck, as though to reassure his housemother.

"Who is carrying the watermelon?" asked Kyle.

Ben laughed, "We don't got a watermelon!"

"Our dinner is in our paper sacks," Willy informed Kyle.

"Hmmm. Well, I guess no one is carrying a melon. I was going to go with you if you had a watermelon. What do you have in those sacks?"

"Wanna see?" asked Floyd opening up his sack and placing it so Kyle glanced into the bag and quickly surmised, "Ahhh, a sandwich, an apple, some cookies. Looks good. Maybe I'll go with you after all."

"Nahhh," said Ben. "You gotta go take Miss Morey on a date and *kiss* her." All the boys laughed and Kyle looked as though he had been had.

Dolores stuck her head out of the second story window and called down to Kyle, "I'll be down to rescue you momentarily!"

"I think it's time for us to get on our way," I said. "Let's go, boys. You and Dolores enjoy your wiener roast, Kyle."

"Thank you, I'm sure we will. That is, if no bears come around this time."

"Good luck on that!" We walked past the three Jesse Lee Home buildings, then the Matthews' house, and finally down the rocky road that would lead us to the highway. This route would take us past the community graveyard, and I noticed that grass had overtaken some of the graves, and some of the wooden markers were in bad need of paint.

"Dat where dead people are, huh Mis Sepps?" asked Willy.

"Yes. This is the graveyard." The rest of the boys just silently stared at the graves and walked on by. I wondered what was in their minds at the time. Seven of the eleven boys had lost at least one parent. No doubt death was a mystery to them, but obviously, this was not a time they wanted to talk about that subject.

At the highway, I insisted the boys walk in two's and stay close together. After a short while, we crossed the highway and had to conquer a ditch or two, as we proceeded towards the railroad bridge. Once the bridge was in sight, the boys quickly scattered and found their favorite eating spots, perching themselves on the railroad ties that protruded out from under the bridge. Since land was not far beneath them, and it didn't appear any boys could fall into the water, I relaxed. I assumed that Rachel had okayed these chosen spots, and indeed they did look safe. I had brought my camera and took pictures of the boys enjoying their sack suppers in the early evening sunshine. After eating, they walked along the stream and watched for the salmon returning to where their lives had begun.

"I shoulda brought a fishing pole!" said Ben. "Look at that big fish!"

"Where?" came the shouts of the others as they went running to Ben at the side of the stream.

"Yeah," commented Chuck. "We shoulda!"

More and more of the salmon appeared. Some with hooked noses and bright red bodies. "That's how they look just before they lay their eggs and die," informed Chuck to the rest of the group.

"Gees! They are gettin' so thick, we could almost pick'em up with our hands," cried Kurt.

"Wanna try?" asked Max sticking his hand in the water.

"No, we're not going to take fish home today, Max. Get out of the water."

"Aw, shucks, Miss Epps. I almost had one."

"We're not prepared to take fish back with us today. Maybe another time."

"Won't last much longer. These fish are nearly dead," said Chuck.

"Nearly dead? Look, some of'em have their skin torn on the sides," added Kurt.

"Probably tore it on the rocks trying to get up stream," continued Chuck.

"Nahhh, I don't want doz dead fish," announced Willy.

"How else you gonna eat'em, Willy?" teased Jeff.

"Yeah, you gonna eat'em alive, Willy?" added Jack.

"I not gonna eat'em," and Willy walked away from the bank and the flowing water.

"We'd better get back, boys. It will be almost bed time by the time we arrive."

"Just a little while longer, Miss Epps. Please," pleaded Max.

"Okay, five more minutes but when I blow the whistle, I want everybody to stop what you are doing and come straight to me." The boys were pleased with that news, and some continued to watch the fish, while others crawled around on the railroad ties under the bridge and dared to jump to the ground. Of course the five minutes passed all too quickly for some, but they knew they had no choice but to go with the group and return. The boys loved getting away from the campus, if only for a brief outing.

On the way back Dale and Alvin walked along side of me quietly. Finally Alvin spoke, "I'm glad we did this, Miss Epps."

"Me too," said Dale.

"You know what, boys?" With a big smile I said, "Me too."

* * *

It was early September and autumn was painting the birch and aspen trees in glorious hues of yellow. Small shrubs showed a touch of red, especially from the wild berry plants growing at all levels of elevation. As far as the eye could see, Mother Nature had become a quick change artist. The fall evening temperatures dropped almost overnight, and the lush greens were changed to brilliant bright yellows and soft oranges. Dolores thought she could almost forgive Seward for all those wet, gloomy days of constant drizzling, summer rain. She likened Seward to the "Ugly Duckling" story and concluded in her thoughts aloud, "If Seward remains this beautiful, this town earns my apology."

"Enjoy it while you can!" came a voice from across the circle of people who were roasting wieners on the beach of Resurrection Bay. Because of the smoke rising between them, Dolores couldn't see the face of the person making the comment. Not that it mattered . . . she didn't know any one in this group of Kyle's acquaintances anyway.

So she replied, "Oh? Why is that?"

Several answers came forth almost simultaneously: "Won't last long!" "It's short." "Beautiful but short!"

"Alas, nothing lasts forever," she sighed. Suddenly a gentle breeze blew the smoke in her direction, and she began to wave her hand rapidly in front of her face. Her eyes watered from the smoke. Dolores jumped to her feet saying, "This smoke is getting to me! I'd better move."

"This smoke is keeping the 'no-see-ums' and the mosquitoes off of you," said Kyle grinning jovially.

"What's a 'no-see-um'?" asked someone from across the circle.

"They are tiny gnats. Their bite will leave a big knot on your skin for days if you are sensitive to their sting," Kyle replied.

"Yeah, they are so tiny you can hardly see them," added a female voice. "That's why the locals call them 'no-see-ums'."

Another person spoke up, "One raised a lump on my forehead the size of a walnut in a matter of minutes recently."

"Did the swelling last long?" asked Dolores.

"About a week."

"Some choice we have here . . . watery eyes from the smoke or welts from the insects!" lamented Dolores.

"Here, have some bug dope," offered Kyle. "It may smell unpleasant, but this will keep the bugs off while you enjoy the prettiest place in the world this time of year."

Dolores reluctantly accepted the oily, smelly, liquid and smeared it on her skin. "And of course you wouldn't be the least bit prejudiced," said Dolores.

"Of course not!" he responded with a big grin. "With our nights beginning to get nippy, we won't need bug dope much longer. Thank goodness."

"And when we drive up to Anchorage on my next day off, I'm sure we'll be in for a treat with all of these fall colors," Dolores remarked.

"You bet! We'll see beauty for miles and miles," assured Kyle.

She smiled at Kyle realizing that his friendship, and the fact that he owned a car, was giving her opportunities that were not readily available to most of the other staff at Jesse Lee. She was glad Mr. Melroy was so persistent in making her acquaintance on the train. She rarely saw him in Seward. But she guessed his intended mission was accomplished; so he stepped aside to allow whatever relationship might grow between his friend Kyle and her.

"Yep, the views along Turnagain Arm are spectacular this time of year," Kyle continued.

In the silence around the fire, everyone seemed to have conjured up a view of the Seward Highway winding through the colorful mountains and dropping down to sea level along Turnagain Arm. At that point, the road paralleled the railroad tracks into Anchorage. Travelers by train or car had fantastic views.

"I saw some of this route by train at the beginning of the summer, as I traveled from Anchorage to Seward. It is indeed something to brag about, and that was well before the colors of autumn arrived."

"Once you drink that in, you'll have a memory of Alaska you'll never lose," pronounced Kyle.

Dolores simply smiled.

"Okay, now that we have established that fall is beautiful in Alaska, why don't we go around this circle and discover what brought each of you to Seward?" suggested Kyle as a way of introducing each to Dolores.

A young woman wearing no make-up and her hair pulled straight back and tied into a ponytail with a small ribbon spoke up. "Since I'm sitting next to you, I guess you want me to start. I'm from Illinois. I heard there were jobs available up here. That's why I came. Haven't found much more than a waitress job yet, but I'm looking."

"Me too," said the young man next to her. "I'm looking for a job."

"Have you tried the docks for longshoring?" asked Kyle.

"Yeah, I might get on there when the next freighter comes in."

"That's how a lot of young men get started in Alaska," he assured him.

The next one answered, "I'm a nurse and I came up to work at the TB Sanatorium."

"I'm also a nurse. I came up to work at the hospital," was the next person.

And so it went around the circle with most speaking of jobs or would-be jobs bringing them to Alaska, until the question reached a swarthy fellow wearing dark clothing. Up to this point, he had spoken very little or at most in monosyllables, when it seemed necessary to utter any words at all. He cleared his throat, as if to postpone his presentation. "I'm from the southwestern United States." Without any notable expression on his face he continued, "I'm staying in Alaska until they elect a new sheriff in my county." No one laughed. There was an awkward pause. It was obvious no further information would be forthcoming. Was this man serious? Did they dare think he might be a fugitive from justice? Surely someone in the group would shed some light on this man. But no one did, as the question moved around the circle.

In the car returning to Jesse Lee, Dolores asked Kyle, "Who was that fellow who said he was waiting for a new sheriff to be elected?"

"I don't know him. He came with one of the women."

"Do you think he was serious?"

"Might be. Alaska attracts all kinds. We learn to ask as few questions as possible. Most figure if someone's background is questionable, as long as that individual is causing no one harm, it's none of our business."

"Hmmm, that's very benevolent of you, but I'm afraid my curiosity wouldn't allow for that kind of attitude to hang around very long."

* * *

John hollered, "You ready to go, Betty Jane?" He had pulled the truck around to the staff cottage, and I quickly climbed into the cabin of the truck. "You bet! So, where are we going, John?"

"Oh, just to a few choice spots that I want to keep in my memory of this summer in Alaska. I'd like to show them to you." I found myself being taken on a tour of the outlying roads around Seward. Although there weren't many, each had a special beauty and a designated area that John wanted to share. Sometimes John would park the truck, and we would walk about enjoying the displays of nature. As we talked, we both sensed the timing for our acquaintance was all wrong. We each seemed to regret that we crossed each other's paths in life so briefly. I was beginning to feel a nippiness in the air, as night came on. John noticed me slightly shivering. "You cold?" he asked, as he put his arm around me. Immediately I felt John's warmth in more ways than one, and it pleased me. I allowed his arm around me, as we walked back to the truck.

"I think we'll be more comfortable inside the truck. Shall we?" he asked.

"Yes, I think you are right." John helped me to climb up into the Jesse Lee Home truck. He must have noticed the difference in our heights. I was exactly 5' 2¾" to his six feet. Long legs were a definite advantage when climbing into a truck, and I didn't have them. Once I was settled in the passenger seat, John walked to the driver's side, opened the door, and easily thrust his six foot frame up into the cab of the truck. Without hesitation he pulled me to him, putting his arm around me again.

"Don't want you to have memories of freezing to death on your one date with John Street," he grinned.

"No, that would never do. Although I might make history, as the first person to freeze to death in Alaska in nonfreezing temperatures."

"Well, we just can't take that chance," he said, as he snuggled closer. I responded with a smile and looked up into his face, just inches away. Suddenly it appeared he was going for a kiss. Kissing John farewell seemed the thing to do. It was a warm, affectionate kiss, that seemed to regret the future would hold nothing further for us. Thus, it appeared John was sealing his Jesse Lee Home experience with that special kiss, and would soon return to Texas to finish his education to prepare for the ministry. I, on the other hand, would continue with the challenges that lay ahead for me at Jesse Lee Home.

END OF BOOK ONE

Jesse Lee Home with fireweed in foreground. Photo from Rachel Yokel's collection.

Dear Reader,

It will give me much pleasure to hear from you. I welcome your comments. My blog is bettyarnett.com and my email is ishka@gci.net.

Betty Epps Arnett